The
Quad Plus

The Quad Plus

Towards a
Shared Strategic
Vision for the
Indo-Pacific

EDITORS
WALTER LOHMAN
LT GENERAL RAVI K SAWHNEY
ANDREW DAVIES
IPPEITA NISHIDA

wisdom
tree

In association with

The Heritage Foundation

The Tokyo Foundation
Developing Policy. Investing in People. Transforming Society.

ASPI
AUSTRALIAN
STRATEGIC
POLICY
INSTITUTE

Yuchengco Center
De La Salle University
Manila

ISBN 978-81-8328-395-3

Published by
Wisdom Tree
4779/23, Ansari Road
Darya Ganj, New Delhi-110 002
Ph.: 23247966/67/68
wisdomtreebooks@gmail.com

Printed in India

Contents

Editor's Note

In May 2007, mid-level foreign ministry officials of the US, Japan, Australia and India met on the margins of the ASEAN Regional Forum (ARF) in Manila to explore the potential for a quadrilateral strategic dialogue. Amid misgivings from the partner nations' foreign policy establishments, changes in political circumstances, and most importantly, protests from the People's Republic of China (PRC), the initiative soon withered.

The concept, however, has not gone away. There is something commonsensical about four vibrant, committed democracies spanning the Indo-Pacific coming together to discuss their common strategic security interests. Three of the countries are formal treaty allies, and India, although steadfastly independent in outlook, is engaged in interlocking dialogues which ultimately include all four.

Since 2007, coordination among these four nations—as well as other like-minded neighbours—has come to make even more sense.

In the intervening seven years, the spectrum of opinion in all four capitals about the appropriate management of the China-challenge has shifted in the direction of concern. Officials have yet to abandon hope of the PRC becoming a cooperative 'responsible stakeholder' in the international system. Indeed, it remains the goal of all concerned. The record of late, however, from the PRC's activity on India's northern border to its attempts to physically alter the territorial status quo in the East and South China Seas has put a much higher premium on hedging against risk. In turn, hedging speaks to the need for allies and partners pooling analytical resources and exploring areas of cooperation to address common threats. The aim is not a strategy for containment of China. That is not a sensible goal in any case given the many interdependencies between all the countries involved. Rather, the aim is for the perspectives represented in the quadrilateral dialogue to produce a coherent approach to managing the new power balances in the Indo-Pacific region.

Political environments in all four countries have also changed in ways to support dialogue. Each new government is seized with geopolitically related security concerns and looking for solutions. Japan's new prime minister was the author of the quadrilateral concept during his former turn in office. Australia's prime minster has been critical of a previous government's withdrawal from the dialogue. The approach of India's new government to the PRC, particularly on border issues, is also firming up. And for its part, the US has in many ways very publicly reaffirmed its bipartisan commitment to Asia by way of its 'pivot' or 'rebalance'.

For all this convergence of circumstances, unfortunately, the PRC's objections to the Quad have in all likelihood not disappeared. Genuine or calculated, anticipated cries of 'containment' by PRC officials and government-controlled media may still have the effect of deterring consultations.

All of these factors contribute to the imperative of restarting Quad dialogue at the Track II or non-government level. Argument for officially restarting the Quad and recommendations for handling diplomatic fallout from the PRC can be made in a different time and place. In the interim, non-government agendas can be developed. Governments can determine whether and how to avail themselves of the analysis at such time as they choose, whether in conjunction with a restart of the official Quad or piecemeal.

In 2013, The Heritage Foundation, The Tokyo Foundation, Vivekananda International Foundation (VIF) and the Australian Strategic Policy Institute (ASPI) came together in Canberra, Australia to develop such an agenda. In an effort to expand the dialogue to other democracies with a strategic stake, they extended the partnership to the Yuchengco Center at De La Salle University in Manila and called the resulting dialogue the 'Quad Plus'. Scholars from all five partner nations participated, as did a scholar from Indonesia. Delegation leaders included Masahiro Akiyama, President of the The Tokyo Foundation; Dr James Jay Carafano, Vice President of The Heritage Foundation's Davis Institute for International Studies; Dr Andrew Davies, Director of Research from ASPI; and Ambassador Kanwal Sibal, Dean of VIF's Centre for International Relations and Diplomacy. The day-and-a-half long discussion revolved around several papers prepared by select participants, discussants assigned to critique the papers, and roundtable discussions. The papers, as revised, follow in this volume. The plan of the partner organisations is to continue the Track II dialogue indefinitely on an annual basis and rotate the 'plus' role among other democratic stakeholders in the region.

The official quadrilateral dialogue was abandoned after 2007. Perhaps, it was an idea ahead of its time. Circumstances have developed such that today, few in Quad Plus country capitals would argue that some manner of coordination and consultation among them is not desirable. At the very least, we would hope for an intensification of that process and that our private dialogues can help prudently feed it.

Walter Lohman
Director, Asian Studies Center
The Heritage Foundation

CHAPTER 1

The Value of the Quad Plus

Kanwal Sibal

The Quad Plus dialogue is a useful platform to exchange views on Asian security issues. The first attempt to establish this dialogue under Japanese Prime Minister Shinzo Abe's first term faltered because of China's opposition and Australia's decision to back away from it. It is not clear how enthused the US was about this move. India was ambivalent, neither clearly for or against.

The rise of China and its implications for Asian security was the driving reason for proposing the Quad arrangement, and remains so. China's claim that its rise will be peaceful and that any parallel with the rise of Germany that triggered World War I would be mistaken, can be legitimately doubted, though the nature of the conflict that may arise may be different. China's demographic, territorial, economic and growing military size makes its rise almost unique in history. Its 1.3 billion population, its status as the second largest economy in the world and the world's biggest exporter, with foreign exchange reserves of USD 3.7 trillion, coupled with the sense of historical grievances that it carries and its territorial claims on land and sea affecting several neighbours, are enough reasons why other countries need to be wary of its rise. If China acquires more and more political, economic and military power, it will use it to advance its interests in the natural course of things. This will inevitably be at the cost of the interests of others in different degrees, irrespective of the rhetoric of 'win-win' situations.

China's political system adds to the concerns, as it is opaque and decision-making processes are clouded in mystery. For a major global player like China to have such a centralised political system that is intolerant of any dissent against the Communist Party, and in which the relationship between the armed forces and the political authority is not clear to outsiders, is worrisome in itself.

China has begun to flex its muscles, becoming more 'self-assertive'. It has drawn the nine-dash line in the South China Sea (SCS) arbitrarily, it has raised tensions over the Senkakus in the East China Sea with Japan, stoking them further by declaring an Air Defence Identification Zone (ADIZ) in this area that also extends to these islands. It has already forcibly occupied the Scarborough Shoal claimed by the Philippines. China's leadership has made it clear that on the issues of territorial sovereignty it will not compromise.

The Quad Plus forum, therefore, makes sense as all the participating countries share concerns, from their individual perspectives, about the unpredictable consequences of China's rise. The US is not an Asian power geographically, but politically, economically and, above all, militarily, it is very much so. It has several military alliances in the region, with troops on the ground in some countries, a powerful naval presence and membership of Asian security and economic institutions. At one level, it acts as a stabilising factor, deterring use of force by any powerful country to change the territorial realities on the ground. In any case, if the 'Indo-Pacific' concept is accepted as valid geopolitically, then the US, with its Pacific territories, becomes integral to Asian security.

While concerns about China are central to Quad members, the diplomatic need exists not to project the Quad as an anti-China group, given that all the countries involved have extensive ties with China and are committed to a policy of engaging, not containing it. The Quad can be, therefore, projected as a group of democracies seeking to strengthen their ties with each other on the basis of shared values. Indirectly, this helps to isolate China as a non-democratic state and erode its political standing.

Japanese Prime Minister Shinzo Abe has been quite blunt about democratic Japan, believing in universal values, seeking strategic ties with other democratic partners to counter the Chinese naval threat in the East China and South China Seas. He has textually said that he 'envisages a strategy whereby Australia, India, Japan, and the US state of Hawaii form a diamond to safeguard the maritime commons stretching from the Indian Ocean to the Western Pacific', adding that he was 'prepared to invest, to the extent possible, Japan's capabilities in this security diamond'. Other countries have not adopted the logic and the language of Prime Minister Abe, though his concerns about Chinese claims to the South China Sea converting it into a 'Lake Beijing' for stationing Chinese nuclear submarines equipped with long range missiles and parading its aircraft carrier there to intimidate its neighbours would have resonance with them.

The democracy argument for bringing the Quad countries together, while understandable in the context of the political challenge Japan has to face in justifying the expansion of its strategic horizons—keeping in mind its historical baggage—carries limited conviction with countries like India. We have been democratic and pluralist ever since our independence, but this has not paid us any notable dividends in our relations with Western democracies, especially the US, all these decades. On the contrary, we have been sanctioned, denied technologies and strategically damaged severely.

The Quad countries, for instance, have sanctioned or isolated us on non-proliferation and missile issues; the US has armed Pakistan against us and pressured us on Kashmir and human rights issues. It has strategically worked with China against us, including overlooking Chinese nuclear and missile transfers to Pakistan. Even now it is not willing to confront China on its latest nuclear cooperation projects in Pakistan in violation of its NSG commitments. Its efforts to reach out to the Taliban as part of its Afghanistan withdrawal strategy, despite the odious ideology of this politico-religious force, and seeking the support of the Pakistani military for facilitating this, is against Indian interests. How do we then reconcile our democracies working together in Western Pacific against the China threat and not working together against the combined China–Pakistan threat to India from land and sea?

India, also, has some reticence with regard to democracies clubbing together politically against non-democracies. While we believe in democracy and cherish our own, we have serious reservations about using democracy as a political instrument to target other countries and seek to impose democracy on them by bringing about regime change if necessary. We have seen how value-based foreign policy has created a moral and political basis to intervene in the internal affairs of countries, including militarily. Iraq, Libya and Syria are disturbing examples of the terrible consequences of such policies for societies that were supposed to benefit from these interventions. Because it is practically impossible to base a foreign policy on rigid adherence to principles, we see double standards in the application of a values-based foreign policy, which further erodes its legitimacy. Adversaries are targeted for the very reasons for which friends are spared.

The US has a huge economic and financial relationship with China. Chinese political and social values have nothing in common with Western values, and lack of democracy in China has not stood in its way of becoming the US's largest economic partner. China openly rejects Western style democracy and its human rights record is abominable. China is also Japan's valuable economic partner, even though China and Japan do not share democratic values. Australia's largest two-way trading partner is China and India's largest trading partner in goods is China too. Should one, therefore, pay all that much attention to 'democratic values' in our relationship with China, given the inconsistencies in what we say and what we do?

Within the Quad, India's relationship with the US has got transformed into a strategic relationship after the India–US nuclear deal. India and the US have an extraordinarily wide-ranging bilateral agenda, covering the fields of counterterrorism, defence, energy, trade, agriculture, education etc. India's military exercises with the US outnumber those with all the other countries combined together. Defence ties have expanded, with India acquiring USD 9 billion worth of arms from the US in the last six years. The US regards India as a key participant in its pivot or rebalancing towards Asia. Of late, the momentum of ties has slowed down, but a solid basis of ties has been created for the future. India is comfortable with the US presence in the Indo-Pacific region.

India, however, has doubts about the underlying reality of the US pivot towards Asia that seeks to hedge against the expansion of Chinese power in the Western Pacific. America's relationship with China is so intense, with a virtual financial fusion between the two, that one can doubt US willingness and capacity to circumscribe China's rise or substantially pare its aggressive edges. Can the US risk serious tensions with China when so much is at stake for it in that relationship? China can take advantage of its rising strength vis-à-vis the US by challenging the US strategically in the Western Pacific incrementally, staying always below the level of open confrontation or crossing a threshold that would oblige the US to react. The US will always counsel restraint and moderation to China and remind it of its defence obligations to countries in the region, in the hope that the Chinese will listen and limit their geo-strategic ambitions. But if at a certain point in time ahead, China begins to loom larger and the US finds its power in the region being increasingly challenged, will the US settle for a G-2, which is the underlying sense of President Xi Jinping's concept of a new great power relationship between the two countries?

India would have problems with that eventuality. Already the US, under Presidents Bill Clinton and Barack Obama has overlooked India's security concerns vis-à-vis China and proposed working together for peace and stability in South Asia, a proposition to which India reacted very adversely. India also notes that the US wants to rope India into its rebalancing policy focussed on the Western Pacific, ignoring security threats to India from Tibet and through Pakistan, not to mention China's 'string of pearls' strategy in the Indian Ocean involving Myanmar, Bangladesh, Sri Lanka, Maldives and Pakistan.

The India–Japan relationship holds great promise. India fits into Japanese Prime Minister Abe's vision of expanding Japan's strategic horizon. Japan already has an alliance relationship with the US. It is close to Australia and the ties are reinforced by the close ties both have with the US and the West. The current Australian Prime Minister considers Japan its closest friend in Asia. Japan is Australia's number two trading partner. It has strong ties with Association of Southeast Asian Nations (ASEAN). It is now active in Myanmar.

India, however, has not been a priority country for Japan either as an economic partner or, even less so, as a political partner. This has changed in recent years, with the two countries establishing a global and strategic partnership. Japan is the only country with which India has instituted a 2+2 dialogue, comprising the defence and foreign ministries on both sides. A practice of annual summits has been institutionalised. A trilateral political dialogue with the participation of the US has also been put in place. A strategic piece that has to be put in place yet is an India–Japan civil nuclear agreement, the prospects for which seem to be improving.

Japan is promoting the sale of its amphibious aircraft US-2 to India, but as a non-military platform, although India would have value for the aircraft in its naval version. India and Japan have held naval exercises in the Indian Ocean and off Okinawa, the latter in a trilateral format with the US. India has been reticent about holding trilateral exercises in the Indian Ocean with US and Japan out of concern that it may be seen as India moving into an alliance framework. This inhibition has to be shed, particularly in view of China's systematic encircling of India and eroding our power in the neighbourhood by expanding its ties and presence in South Asia. Any expanded strategic vision of Japan has to have India as new ground to cultivate strategically. By virtue of its demographic, geographic, economic and military size, India is the only country that can counter China in the long term, even on its own. With Japan's readiness to invest in India's infrastructure and manufacturing sector, it can play a very positive role in building India's economic capacity, a role India would greatly welcome.

The weak leg of the Quad group from India's perspective has been Australia, though here too the complexion of the relationship has improved a great deal in recent years. Discussions on Australian uranium sales for India's power plants are progressing well. Why Australia should have been reticent to sell uranium after the India–US nuclear deal and the NSG exemption for India remains unclear, especially as uranium sales to China are permitted. Trade volumes have gone up, reaching close to USD 20 billion in 2011-12. Indian investment in Australia is growing.

In the light of Chinese claims, India has concerns about freedom of navigation in the South China Sea and has called for observance of the international conventions on the law of the sea.

Chinese objections to oil exploration blocks offered by Vietnam to India's Oil and Natural Gas Corporation Ltd (ONGC) as intrusion into areas China claims have naturally irritated India. On the ADIZ, too, India has drawn attention to respect for international law. We have said that any conflict in the South China and East China Seas would roll back the gains to each of the countries in the last forty years. The Indian prime minister has called for a stable maritime environment and has welcomed 'the collective commitment by the concerned countries to abide by and implement the 2002 Declaration on the Conduct of Parties in the South China Sea and to work towards the adoption of a code of conduct in the South China Sea on the basis of consensus.' We have emphasised the importance of upholding the existing international law on maritime security. In the larger context of India–ASEAN relations, we have spoken of our strategic partnership's increasing relevance to the political-security space in East Asia. India's foreign minister has said that 'India's naval footprint is essentially that of a net security provider even as it is set to expand'.

India has the diplomatic challenge of sharing concerns of China's neighbours about Chinese maritime claims and at the same time advocate China's inclusion into any regional security architecture, with a view to finding solutions in cooperation with China rather than in confrontation with it.

The Quad Plus has to carefully analyse the position of ASEAN countries on the degree of push-back that needs to be applied collectively on Chinese maritime claims in South China and East China Seas. ASEAN unity on this specific Chinese challenge has to be maintained. ASEAN, however, may not want to be put in a position to have to choose between Japan and China on the territorial dispute between them. The US position remains a key one. It has signalled that the US–Japan Defence Treaty covers the Senkakus, but it has not taken a position on the sovereignty issue, a position that assures

Japan in the immediate, against use of force, but by not rejecting China's legal claims allows the issue to simmer legally. The US is warning China against changing the de facto position by force but is leaving the de jure position open. If the US is not choosing sides, it is because it cannot easily do so, given the breadth of its ties with China and its treaty obligations towards Japan. The existing efforts to balance its interests also enables the US to continue to exercise control over Japan's foreign and defence policies. There are signals, however, that Japanese uncertainty over the US commitment to come to Japan's defence is growing.

China's direct threat to India is much more serious from our point of view than Chinese maritime claims that put it at odds with the US and several ASEAN countries. Unlike in the case of these countries that can collectively counter China's outlandish claims under US wings, India is alone in dealing with the Chinese threat. The US is not a direct party to India's territorial differences with China.

The Quad's relations with Russia require analysis. Russia is also an Asian power; it is a member of the ARF and now of the East Asia Summit. It has a role in defining the Asian Security Architecture. Japan has the strategic option to reach out to Russia to balance the growing Russia–China ties. It can create greater strategic space for itself by exploring options with Russia, which Prime Minister Abe has begun.

All in all, the Quad Plus is a useful platform to analyse the developing situation in East Asia and its organic links to security in the larger Indo-Pacific region.

Ambassador Kanwal Sibal is former Foreign Secretary of India and currently the Dean, Centre for International Relations and Diplomacy at the Vivekananda International Foundation in New Delhi.

CHAPTER 2

Democracy and Regional Security: An Australian Perspective

ANDREW DAVIES

The democracies of the world have mostly agreed on a set of values and norms of behaviour. These have helped underpinning the period of (relative) peace that we have recently been enjoying and have allowed the globalisation of trade that has lifted the living standards of a large number of people.

The countries represented in the Quad Plus meeting share a great many security interests, including the alliances some of us have with the United States (US) under the 'hub and spokes' model. As well, Australia and India—and to an extent Japan and the US— have shared interests in maritime security in the Indian Ocean. As a result, we are all in many ways natural partners. However, for various historical, political, and I dare say strategic reasons, defence and security collaborations between the countries at this meeting are at different stages of exploration and maturity.

Indeed, in the absence of an external driver, there'd be no great imperative for a consolidated view. We'd make our bilateral and multilateral arrangements in our own good time. But with the rise of China as a major but decidedly undemocratic power which seems to have different ideas about the norms under which it wants to operate, we might not have the luxury of working up slowly.

To me the interesting question is the extent to which our various nations are driven by our shared liberal democratic values versus our more narrow national interests when push comes to shove. Of course, those things aren't mutually exclusive—in many ways the values that underpin the world order from which we all prosper are the ones this group shares. In the China context, this argument has been playing out in Australia for the last few years, albeit through a somewhat artificial construct of 'would we choose America or China'. In any way that really matters, Australia chose to hitch itself to the US and its world view decades ago. Last year, the Australian government made its position clear in criticising China for the declaration of an Air Defence Identification Zone over the Senkaku Islands—explicitly supporting Japan and the US in the process.

But that's not to say that successive Australian governments have taken identical approaches to our interactions with China and with our democratic friends. While all have been in the 'friends of Australia, New Zealand, United States (ANZUS)' camp, there have been changes in both the rhetoric and activity about participating in a wider 'arc of democracies'. Changes of government have seen Australia at various times more or less willing to align itself with other like-minded countries—and to be seen and heard to be doing so.

Looking forward, the potential costs and benefits of such alignment might both be greater than has been the case previously. As China's power increases without a significant shift in its political approach, the potential threat to the existing order grows. And so, too, does China's ability to harm other nation's interests if its revisionism is denied. At any given decision point, Australia's government will have to weigh those factors against each other. The other nations here will have to do the same. Our calculus will depend on a number of factors, including geography, economics and values.

And we all have our local interests that might not be equally shared with our democratic friends. For example, Australia has a much greater stake in the stability of The Solomon Islands and Timor Leste than do the other Quad members. And, in practical terms, Australia has no stake in the ownership of the Senkaku/Diaou Islands. What we do have, however, is an interest in seeing the dispute resolved by means consistent with the established international order.

Influential Australian thinkers like Hugh White advocate an Australian policy line that is more 'neutral' between Washington and Beijing and, while White's influence has probably diminished with the change of government, there's sensitivity within the Australian polity about the potential economic impact of a substantial falling out with Beijing. Those fears are probably overstated—after all, markets are global and China needs to source its raw materials from somewhere—but they do play into Australian thinking.

AUSTRALIA AND THE QUAD

The idea of a quadrilateral security arrangement between the US, Australia, Japan and India is an idea that goes back at least a decade now. It reached its formal zenith during 2007, when the first formal Quadrilateral Security Dialogue (QSD) was held and there were extensive military exercises among the four countries. Australia signed up to the QSD under Prime Minister John Howard—long a strong supporter of the notion of a concert of democracies.

Around the same time, Australia and Japan signed a 'Joint Declaration on Security Cooperation' in March 2007. The aim was to create mechanisms by which we could work together 'to respond to new security challenges and threats, as they arise' and 'create a comprehensive framework for the enhancement of security cooperation' between the two countries. As a sign of things to come, at the time of the signing of the Joint Declaration by the Howard government, the then Australian Opposition Leader (and future Prime Minister), Kevin Rudd, supported enhanced security cooperation with Japan, but opposed a mutual defence pact, saying that 'to do so at this stage may unnecessarily tie our security interests to the vicissitudes of an unknown security policy future in North East Asia'.

Australia withdrew from the Quadrilateral after the election of the Rudd government, and it's worth exploring the thinking of that government about Asia-Pacific security in a little more detail, because it illustrates some of the difficult issues we need to grapple with. It was around that time that the extent to which Australia wants to become enmeshed in North Asian security became a lively topic for national discussion—something that continues today in various forms.

To the extent that we are able to divine the thinking of the Rudd government (which in terms of foreign policy was in no small way also the thinking of the Prime Minister himself), there was an acute awareness of the significance of the rise of China. Rudd certainly didn't view that development as a benign one. In a conversation with US Secretary of State Hillary Clinton, he described himself as a 'brutal realist on China' and explained the mooted development of Australian naval power—including a doubling of the submarine fleet—as a response to increasing Chinese power projection capabilities. In effect, Australia was committing to bolster Western naval power in the Pacific region.

So, Australian thinking in the 2007-08 period reflected exactly the tensions I described in the introduction. We saw the rise of authoritarian China as a threat that required a military hedging strategy, and we were looking to the US and Japan to assist with our security. But at the same time we recognised that there was a downside risk in committing too deeply to North Asian security.

This reservation was probably heightened by apprehension about the durability of the American commitment to the region. This was all pre-rebalance, and the US was in the process of extricating itself from Iraq and was still deeply involved in Afghanistan.

I think it's fair to say that the rebalance (nee pivot) announcement in late 2011 represented a moment of relief for Australia, and to most other friends and allies in the region. The effect here was probably heightened by President Barack Obama choosing Canberra as the location for a major speech on US Asia-Pacific policy. Kevin Rudd again provided a snapshot of a school of thought in Australia when he commented that, 'Without [the pivot], there was a danger that China, with its hard line, realist view of international relations, would conclude that an economically exhausted US was losing its staying power in the Pacific.'

I haven't mentioned India much in this section. That's because Australia/India security arrangements remain much less advanced than the well-established Australia/United States alliance and the deepening relationship with Japan. I think that reflects two strategic fundamentals. Firstly, India's geography means that its primary maritime domain is far from the increasingly fraught waters of north Asia. The Indian Ocean doesn't contain the contested and crowed spaces that the Western Pacific does. Its sea lines of communication are important, but it's really the bottlenecks at either end that are most significant. Literally and metaphorically, there's more room to move. Secondly, India itself has been more diffident to any alignment with major powers than Australia and Japan have been. Tokyo and Canberra signed on to the American camp at the San Francisco conference more than half a century ago, while India sat out the Cold War as a non-aligned state. There's been no compelling strategic reason for India to move much closer to the Western camp, so it hasn't. The rise of China may be changing that, but the pace has been modest to date.

In fact, strategic and geographic distance is a very good explanatory framework for the dynamics of the Quad. Of the three 'other' members of the Quad, Japan has the greatest motivation for making stronger security arrangements with like-minded countries for the simple reason that it is the country most in 'the firing line'. Chinese thinking about the second island chain is clearly more worrying for a country that forms part of that chain than it is for those of us further away. Australia has the luxury of distance, which probably explains why we've equivocated more about our relationships with Washington and Beijing.

UNITED STATES' SECURITY POLICY AND THE AIRSEA BATTLE CONCEPT

With China now the world's number two economy, and a nuclear power with rapidly increasing conventional strength, the rest of us have a limited ability to resist its efforts to assert itself. The power, reach and willingness to engage with the US are likely to be the lynchpins of any strategy of organised democratic resistance to Chinese assertiveness. So, two of the key questions become: (1) What is the US' strategy, and (2) What are the roles of America's friends and allies in that strategy?

For now, one of the major policy challenges for Australia and Japan (and for other countries in the region) is how we should respond—individually and collectively—to the US pivot/rebalancing now underway and the accompanying development of strategic and military concepts. It's clearly in our collective interests for the US to remain deeply engaged in the region. But we need to understand the American strategy and how we are expected to contribute, and—when necessary—be prepared to push back if we make the judgement that the cost/benefit calculus doesn't suit our interests.

I'm a military analyst, so I'll focus on the military aspects of American strategy. The most important of these is the 'AirSea Battle'

(ASB) concept, which has become the most visible sign of efforts by the US military to readjust its military doctrine to deal with the growing anti-access/area denial (A2AD) challenge posed by China's sophisticated new anti-ship and air defence systems. I'll note here that A2AD might not be the only problem we're faced with in the future—Chinese power projection capabilities are now growing. It's increasingly the case that it's not just a problem of working out how to defeat Chinese access capabilities, but of how to prevent Chinese forces from projecting their own power well out into the second island chain and beyond. China's development today of aircraft carriers and nuclear submarines suggests that we'll look back one day and see A2AD as phase one of a much more ambitious military development process.

As a Center of Strategic and Budgetary Assessment (CSBA) report noted: 'AirSea Battle is not a US-only concept. Allies such as Japan and Australia, and possibly others, must play important enabling roles in a stable military balance'. This raises some important strategic considerations for our defence planning, and it potentially makes it hard for America's allies to maintain a line that they're not part of a strategy of limiting Chinese power.

At least in the public domain, we know relatively little about ASB. But we do know that the American thinking includes a layered approach to defeating A2AD, and there several aspects that will potentially impinge on Australia and Japan's force structures and/or doctrine development, and provide Indian naval power potentially a role to play as well. Alternatively, the other Quad countries might be forced to decide what they *aren't* prepared to do. The ASB components of most significance in this respect are:

- the hardening of bases in North Asia (especially South Korea, Japan and Guam)
- a 'defence in depth' approach of dispersing US forces across a wider area—which is already taking effect in Australia and

could expand to some of the potential 'plus' elements of the Quad Plus.

- tactics and technologies to disrupt the command, control and ISR capabilities of the People's Liberation Army (PLA)
- deep strike capabilities against distant targets
- distant blockade operations against shipping traffic to and from China.

The first two of these activities are relatively easy to implement and can be done on a bilateral basis with the US. Agreements on the hardening of bases or the hosting of US forces are bilateral matters for the US and its allies and partners to discuss among themselves. But the last three of the dot points above are serious undertakings indeed, and would require a great deal of commitment on behalf of America's allies if they were to participate. In short, any American partner in ASB would need to be prepared to participate in a war with China. It would certainly be difficult to make serious preparations in force structure, training and doctrine consistent with participation in ASB and maintain a fiction that there was no intent to militarily constrain China.

Again, individual country's enthusiasm for participation in ASB will depend on the calculus of costs and benefits. And, also as before, it's likely that geography will play a role in shaping the assessment of those costs and benefits. For Japan, there's a finer line between Chinese A2AD and power projection than there is for Australia. For India, the sea lines for trade to and from China through the Indian Ocean would become significant in a 'distant blockade' scenario, but Chinese land forces across its northern borders will probably remain the most significant element of PLA power.

WHAT DOES QUAD PLUS SECURITY COOPERATION LOOK LIKE?

That brings us to the practical question of what Quad Plus cooperation might look like. Again, I'll confine my comments to the military space, but obviously any such move would need to be in support of a wider strategy and be accompanied by diplomatic and economic approaches working together to minimise the opportunities for the liberal democratic order to be chipped away at.

I'll discuss what *might* be done, with the caveat that it doesn't necessarily follow that it *should* be done. In approximate increasing degree of complexity and/or sensitivity, areas for collaborative military work can be broadly classified as follows.

LOW COMMITMENT
* humanitarian and disaster relief capabilities
* collaborative security activities, such as anti-piracy patrols and counter terrorism
* collaboration on cyber defence.

These are really 'low hanging fruit' and most of our countries already have cooperative programmes in place or under development. Examples include multilateral efforts to combat naval piracy, to which Australia, India, Japan, the US (and China) have contributed warships, military exercises to build confidence and experience across regional militaries and humanitarian and disaster relief operations. As well, there are developing relationships in the area of cyber security and network defence. Those are all positive developments, and I'm sure we'll see more of them. But they're mostly 'second order' security matters—with the exception of cyber security—and are thus less challenging to develop than 'first order' security relationships involving the top end military capabilities and the more difficult issues thrown up by the geopolitics of the Asia-Pacific region and beyond.

MEDIUM COMMITMENT
* military exercises designed to build interoperability and warfighting ability
* collaboration on the development of cooperative military capabilities. Examples might include submarine technology and ballistic missile defence

The medium issues are diplomatically workable and more can be done in those areas. While their intent won't go unnoticed in Beijing, there's enough plausible deniability about the ultimate aims to make it palatable to most likely participants.

HIGH COMMITMENT

- development of capabilities and doctrine designed to function within the US 'AirSea Battle' model
- collaboration on sensitive 'asymmetric' capabilities, such as cyber warfare and electronic attack.

The high commitment activities raise the stakes for would-be participants and would effectively signal that they had voted firmly to be part of the US camp in strategic competition with China. As such, these steps would require much more internal discussion. Because they are the highest impact activities, they are also the ones that carry the greatest risk of generating a 'self-fulfilling prophecy'—treating China as an adversary is most likely to ensure that it becomes one. But I worry less about that than I used to—China's own activities and inclinations are making it increasingly clear that it is willing to step up into that role!

CONCLUSION

The Asia-Pacific security landscape is changing in ways that make it more complex—and in some ways more dangerous, as strategic competition between the established major powers and the rising power of the People's Republic of China (PRC) deepens. The American response to the challenge being posed is in many ways still a 'work in progress' and some of the more aggressive notions entering the public domain might be put aside as a more nuanced approach to the 'Asian Century' emerges. But there is still a question as to whether this century will—like the second half of the last— be dominated by internationalist liberal democratic free economy principles, or whether the landscape will be significantly changed by a new approach from China.

Australia, India, Japan and the other nations of the Asia-Pacific need to think hard about both the expectations that the US might have of us, and the benefits and costs of a cooperative approach to maintaining the established world order. Some of the options described here are 'easy'—they can readily be justified and don't have too much downside risk. Others would increase the stakes and certainly won't be appreciated in Beijing—but those are the ones most likely to have a real impact (for better or worse). The trick for us all will be to weigh the costs and benefits and decide which we want to pursue.

Andrew Davies is Director of Research and Senior Analyst specialising in defence capability, defence industry, submarines, F-35 Joint Strike Fighter, ADF force structure, and ANZUS alliance at the Australian Strategic Policy Institute.

CHAPTER 3

Democracy and
Regional Security in Asia
How Liberal Politics Produce Strategic Stability &
Enhance Regional Cooperation

DANIEL TWINING

Asia is often described as the twenty-first century's cockpit of conflict.[1] Military spending in Asia is now greater than that of Europe.[2] Five of the world's nuclear powers face off in the region stretching from Pakistan to the Korean peninsula. China is developing armed forces that threaten its neighbours and are designed to target unique American vulnerabilities. Beijing is pursuing territorial revisionism at sea and, along its contested border with India, on land. Nationalism is resurgent and is complicating relations not only between China and its neighbours, but between core American allies

---

[1] Friedberg, Aaron. "Ripe for Rivalry: Prospects for Peace in a Multipolar Asia," *International Security* 18, No. 3 (Winter 1993/4), pp. 5-33.

[2] Macdonald, Myra. "Asia's Defense Spending Overtakes Europe's: IISS," *Reuters*, 14 March 2013, http://www.reuters.com/article/2013/03/14/us-security-military-iiss-idUSBRE92D0EL 20130314.

like Japan and South Korea. American staying power is in question given defence budget cuts at home and the practical impossibility of a strategic pivot away from the Middle East, given all its problems.

These dangers, however, are countervailed by equally powerful positive trends. The economic miracle launched by Japan following the Pacific war has spread across East, Southeast, and now South Asia, tying China to its neighbours in deep webs of economic interdependence. The US role in the region is arguably stronger, more diversified, and enjoys greater political support. Demand for American leadership and presence in Asia is rising, not falling. Washington has modernised alliances with old friends like Australia, Japan, and South Korea, and built new partnerships with rising swing states like India. Broadening strategic horizons and growing national capabilities render many Asian powers more capable of contributing to regional security.

Perhaps most importantly, the democratisation of Asia—as powerful a trend as the region's economic modernisation since 1945—has created a thriving community of open societies. This has transformed the regional security dynamic in multiple ways. No longer are internal conflicts and cleavages the primary security challenge to most Asian nations, as they were particularly in South and Southeast Asia until quite recently. Asian societies that are well-governed according to principles of accountability and law generate security not only for their people, but for their region, by exporting stability and prosperity. Democratic states that abide by basic rules at home are more likely to uphold and strengthen them abroad, including by respecting international law and promoting peaceful resolution of conflicts over issues like freedom of the seas. And as shown by the democratic peace that has held in the Atlantic community for nearly seven decades, open societies with elected leaders are better able to cooperate to maintain order within their region and to help uphold it farther afield.

This paper considers how democracy in Asia contributes to regional security—highlighting how good governance is a public good that has dramatic spillover effects for regional order. The point is not to make a philosophical case for democracy as a morally preferable form of government, although of course it is. Nor is the objective to frame the extraordinary diversity and pluralism of Asia around an overly simplistic ideological divide. The goal is rather to explain practically how democracy has enhanced regional security, why supporting democratic development in Asia can contribute to regional peace, and how Asia's progressive powers can further anchor regional stability and prosperity through democratic cooperation.

Given that more people in Asia live under democracy than in any other region, it would in many ways be odd not to single out the democracy variable as one of several that ease alignments, facilitate functional cooperation, and frame common interests in ways that promote peace. Nor should focused consideration of cooperation among Asian democracies somehow neglect or exclude important but repressive states like China and Vietnam, or transitional states like Myanmar. On the contrary, the spillover effects of democratic cooperation in Asia are arguably more important for these nations. They ultimately stand to benefit most from the norms of participatory politics and the democratic peace, given that it is their illiberal political systems which constitute the greatest obstacle to full economic modernisation and genuine security. The ultimate transformation of Asia's remaining authoritarian regimes into more open and free societies could consolidate a regional order based on peaceful cooperation, resolving conflicts over territory, history, and military competition that otherwise risk exploding.

This paper examines how democracy contributes to regional security in Asia across a range of functional areas. These include: Enhancing the internal stability of Asian nations in ways that reinforce regional order; facilitating the US role in the region; strengthening regional institutions; enabling meaningful defence and security coordination; and deepening trade and investment. The paper then assesses the broader implications of democratic security cooperation, including for China.

DEMOCRACY & SOVEREIGN AUTONOMY

For all the talk of China's 'authoritarian stability,' the experience of post-war and post-colonial Asia shows that inclusive and accountable political systems are a greater source of security than is the heavy hand of an unelected state. This is because the mechanisms of democracy and federalism help resolve political and socio-economic conflicts peacefully, creating a more secure state whose institutional legitimacy is not challenged by core social groups within it. Open politics have helped weak or post-colonial developing states graduate from the 'third world security predicament,' in which internal fissures within the state, not external threats, put its sovereignty under greatest strain. Such weak states in turn destabilise their neighbourhoods, including by drawing great powers into their internal conflicts.[3]

Association of Southeast Asian Nations (ASEAN) was established to prevent such great power interventions in Southeast Asia by upholding the norm of non-interference in the internal affairs of member states. But as shown by ASEAN's own history, including the democratisation of its dominant member state, the institution's adoption of a Human Rights Charter, and the way Myanmar's pathologies before its political opening handicapped ASEAN's institutional effectiveness, national sovereignty is more secure when countries are governed well and responsive to their citizenries.

Indonesia provides a striking example of how internal turmoil, civil war, and secessionism under strongman rule have given way to a much more durable internal political settlement under democracy.

---

[3] Ayoob, Mohammed. *The Third World Security Predicament: State-Making, Regional Conflict, and the International System* (Boulder: Lynne Rienner, 1995).

Unlike in the eras of Sukarno and Suharto, political transitions no longer result in mass bloodshed, regions enjoy substantial autonomy rather than pursuing violent secessionist campaigns, the armed forces can focus on external security rather than repressing dissident populations, and internal peace with rule of law has produced broad-based prosperity, transforming democratic Indonesia into a next-generation Brazil, Russia, India, China and South Africa (BRICS).

Whereas Indonesia's democracy grew out of a bottom-up political revolution, Myanmar's top-down political opening was instigated by its ruling generals after decades of repression, stagnation, and active civil war against various armed minority groups produced a failing state. Internal security was degraded by the active resistance of substantial parts of the population, including various ethnic groups and the National League for Democracy, to the regime. External security was diminished by the country's isolation from the West, Myanmar's inability to keep up with prosperous neighbours, its inability to control insurgent groups on its territory operating across national borders, and its penetration by China, creating excessive economic and political dependencies that undermined Myanmar's sovereign autonomy. Myanmar is not yet a democracy, but political and economic liberalisation have begun to resolve each of these problems, strengthening Myanmarese sovereignty and security.

It should not come as any surprise that the principal threats to regional and global security emanating from Asia come from authoritarian China, totalitarian North Korea, and a weakly democratic Pakistan where elected leaders do not control national security policy, creating a witches' brew of risk from proliferation and terrorism. Regional democracies have serious problems, including massive official corruption in India and the Philippines, social polarisation in Thailand, personalised political rivalry along dynastic lines in Bangladesh, a flawed form of majoritarian rule in Malaysia, and restrictions on political opposition rights in Singapore.

For all these problems, none of these countries is projecting insecurities in ways that risk military conflict with neighbours; rather, their internally competitive political systems keep their domestic conflicts bounded and help resolve social cleavages, however imperfectly. To the extent a country like Thailand is unstable, it is because of the weakness of democratic institutions, not their strength. In Asia as elsewhere, sovereignty is more assured through democratic politics than authoritarian control.

FACILITATING THE US ROLE IN ASIA

The democratisation of Asian states has facilitated the US military and diplomatic presence as a regional guarantor of security and stability. In that sense, democracy within Asia has helped to strengthen the American security umbrella that, by diverting competition away from arms racing and military balancing among suspicious neighbours, has made possible the Asian economic miracle. However, it was not always this way.

The US presence and role in post-World War II Asia pre-dates the liberalisation of politics in traditional allies like South Korea, Taiwan, Thailand, and the Philippines. Indeed, the US fought a war against North Korea even before Japan was fully sovereign and while South Korea was under military dictatorship. America committed to Taiwan's defence while the island was under one-party rule. The US waged its war against North Vietnam from bases and supply lines in a Thailand then under authoritarian rule, in defence of a regime in Saigon which was not a democracy. And the biggest American military base in Southeast Asia, at Subic Bay, functioned under Philippine autocracy until that country's democratisation brought to power leaders who asked the US to withdraw its forces.

Nonetheless, democratic politics more recently have made the US presence in Asia more sustainable and diversified. Part of the problem in the Philippines was the popular view that Washington had been too close to strongmen in Manila; now, two decades later, elected leaders have invited American forces to return in missions viewed as legitimate by the Philippine people. There is no question that the US–Republic of Korea alliance is more durable now that South Korea is a vibrant democracy, with American forces no longer in the position of defending an unelected government in Seoul against an unelected government in Pyongyang. Although the military balance across the Taiwan Strait has shifted dangerously in Beijing's favour, it is also clear that democracy strengthens Taiwan's claim to its own identity and more starkly underscores why Washington remains committed to the defence of this free society against unprovoked Chinese aggression.

Asia's mature democracies have seen popular support for partnership with the US grow rather than diminish over time. In Japan, stable majorities support the US alliance; when 'regime change' occurred with the Democratic Party of Japan's (DPJ) displacement of the Liberal Democratic Party (LDP) in 2009, public support for the alliance did not waver even as a prime minister who sought 'equidistance' with China briefly held power, with the result that a set of more pro-alliance politicians ultimately displaced him. American forces are back in Australia as a result of the confidence of this country's elected politicians that public support for what might otherwise be a controversial deployment is firm. In India, it was not an American leader but rather Prime Minister Atal Bihari Vajpayee who first declared in 1998 that India and the US were 'natural allies' not only on account of shared threat perceptions from China and terrorism, but because of their shared values.[4]

Among Southeast Asia's big 'swing states', there is no question that democracy in Indonesia makes that country a better security partner going forward, with American partnership reinforcing the

---

[4]Vajpayee, Atal Bihari. "India, USA, and the World," Remarks by the Prime Minister at the Asia Society, New York City, 28 September 1998, www.asiasociety.org/speeches/vajpayee.html.

country's ability to better secure its sea lanes rather than to repress its people. Indeed, Indonesia has successfully stewarded the Bali Democracy Forum as a way of enhancing regional security by promoting good governance and rule of law. Conversely, a big question mark around US security partnership with Vietnam, whose leaders are like-minded about the China challenge to regional order, is the nature of the regime in Hanoi, whose restrictions on political activity and persecution of peaceful civic opponents will remain a stumbling block to closer military cooperation.

STRENGTHENING REGIONAL INSTITUTIONS

Democracy in Asia also bolsters regional security by strengthening the effectiveness of regional institutions. It is true that there are no all-democratic clubs in Asia, and that regional cooperation has deepened despite a diversity of regime types among member states. But it is also true that the leading powers within most key regional institutions are democracies; that democracies have found it easier to cooperate with each other in regional institutions than with authoritarian states; and that authoritarian regimes have held back the development of Asian regional institutions rather than promoting it. Based on the evidence, the more widespread the democratisation of Asian powers who can effectively concert within regional institutions, the more effective those groupings will be in providing regional public goods.

The debate over the founding membership of the East Asia Summit (EAS) in 2005 was instructive.[5] China's preference was for a closed grouping encompassing the ASEAN states plus itself, Japan, and South Korea—excluding Asia's democratic giant, India, as well as mature democracies Australia and New Zealand. Japan and Singapore led the lobbying campaign to broaden EAS membership out to the ASEAN + 6 format, thereby including the Indo-Pacific democracies

---

[5]Malik, Mohan. "The East Asia Summit: More Discord than Accord," *YaleGlobal Online*, 20 December 2005, http://yaleglobal.yale.edu/content/east-asia-summit-more-discord-accord.

alongside the East and Southeast Asian states. Interestingly, Vietnam, despite its authoritarian regime, was also active in pushing to broaden the grouping to tilt it in the direction of the democracies—not because of its political values, obviously, but because of its interest in preventing Chinese domination of the grouping.

The EAS founding leadership tussle was an example of how political values and national interests intersect. Most Asian states, some less than democratic, naturally felt more comfortable including nations like India and Australia to balance China's weight. More recently, of course, membership in the EAS has broadened out further to include, among other countries, the US, further diluting Chinese influence and diminishing China's interest in promoting EAS as Asia's leading decision-making body.

Despite ASEAN's rhetoric about sovereign non-interference—including the extraordinary sensitivity of member states to the risk of great-power domination—we have seen a similar dynamic play out in other ASEAN-led groupings, including the ASEAN Regional Forum (ARF) and the ASEAN Defense Ministers' Ministerial-Plus (ADMM-Plus) dialogues. These clubs are designed not to keep the Indo-Pacific great powers out of Southeast Asia, but rather to pull them in. They have been promoted by smaller states with an eye on enmeshing great powers in Southeast Asian security in ways that hedge against both domination by any one great power and, concomitantly, the abandonment of Southeast Asia by multiple great powers, subjecting smaller powers to the whims of a regional hegemon.

Institutions like ARF and ADMM-Plus pull countries like the US, Japan, India, and Australia into Southeast Asian affairs in ways that dilute the influence of China and give ASEAN states multiple options for securing their strategic autonomy through extra-regional partnerships. It is not coincidental that the powers Southeast Asian states have sought to enmesh in their region include not only authoritarian China—as a way of socialising it into norms of regional cooperation—but all of the primary Indo-Pacific democracies. China is seen not only as a key trading partner and investor but also as a primary source of potential danger; the big regional democracies are seen as stabilisers whose open and transparent systems render their footprint in Southeast Asia more a source of security than insecurity.

DEFENCE AND SECURITY COOPERATION

Democracy within the principal non-Chinese Indo-Pacific powers has helped catalyse security cooperation between them. Realists might view the deepening of strategic ties between India and Japan, Japan and Australia, India and Australia, and both Japan and India with Southeast Asian powers like Indonesia as classic billiard-ball balancing behaviour that bears no relation to domestic regime type. All these partnerships are unquestionably grounded in national-interest assessments about hedging against Chinese instabilities and providing regional public goods like sea-lane security. But it is instructive that Asian leaders themselves view these partnerships not only in terms of interests, but in terms of common values.

The example of India and Japan is revealing, partly because it is a constellation that does not include the US, Australia, or another 'Western' power, and partly because of how New Delhi has dispensed with its traditional dedication to non-alignment to construct a far-reaching strategic entente with Tokyo. There is certainly a balancing logic to this alignment: As one Indian newspaper recently put it, 'Shinzo Abe wants [a] larger Indian presence in East Asia to check China.'[6] But the way both Indian and Japanese leaders talk about the logic of partnership, it rises above narrow material calculations of power and interest.

---

[6] Chaudhary, Dipanjan Roy. "Shinzo Abe Wants Larger Indian Presence in East Asia to Check China," *Economic Times*, 29 October 2013, http://articles.economictimes.indiatimes.com/2013-10-29/news/43496138_1_pm-abe-indian-parliament-prime-minister-shinzo-abe.

In 2007, Shinzo Abe, then Japan's prime minister, gave a speech to the Indian Parliament in which he emphasised 'the confluence of the two seas'—the Indian and Pacific oceans—tying Japan and India together in this era of globalisation. He stressed that both countries 'share fundamental values such as freedom, democracy, and respect for human rights as well as strategic interests.' And he highlighted how a grand 'Arc of Freedom and Prosperity' connected Japan in the east to India in the south to Europe in the west.[7] Such a network of powerful democracies acting in concert, including the US, could decisively shape the twenty-first century, believes Prime Minister Abe today.

In India, an internal struggle over policy recently has pitted 'China school' officials against those who see strategic advantage in leveraging India's interests in China through partnership with powerful democracies like Japan and the US. During his tenure Prime Minister Manmohan Singh had personally intervened in this debate on the side of constructing a far-reaching strategic partnership with Japan on the basis of a common democratic outlook, just as he personally put his leadership on the line in 2008 to secure passage of a civil-nuclear agreement with the US. In May 2013 in Tokyo, Singh stressed 'shared values and shared interests' in explaining that Indians 'see Japan as a natural and indispensable partner in our quest for stability and peace in the vast region in Asia that is washed by the Pacific and Indian Oceans.' Indeed, 'India and Japan have a shared vision of a rising Asia', one that will protect and extend the 'rise in freedom, opportunity and prosperity' that has occured over the last half century.[8]

---

[7] Baru, Sanjaya. "The Importance of Shinzo Abe," *The Hindu*, 19 December 2012, http://www.thehindu.com/opinion/op-ed/the-importance-of-shinzo-abe/article4214264.ece.

[8] "PM's address to Japan–India Association, Japan–India Parliamentary Friendship League and International Friendship Exchange Council," 28 May 2013, Tokyo, http://pmindia.nic.in/speech-details.php?nodeid=1319.

Beyond bilateral defence and security cooperation, the expansion of like-minded minilateralism among the Indo-Pacific democracies attests to the synergies that arise from security cooperation among democracies with common outlooks. These include:

- The US-Japan-South Korea trilateral, which has continued North Korea-related contingency planning and joint military exercises despite tensions between Seoul and Tokyo over history issues.
- The US-Japan-Australia trilateral, which has effectively merged US–Japan and US–Australia alliance cooperation with the Japan–Australia strategic partnership.
- The US-Japan-India trilateral, pushed hard by Tokyo and at the Track 2 level until it was finally consummated as an official strategic dialogue in 2011, with excellent results.
- The Quadrilateral Partnership of 2006-07 which grew out of the 2004 tsunami relief partnership between the US, Japan, Australia, and India, demonstrating how like-minded, capable democracies can provide tangible public goods in Asia that benefit the entire region.

Beyond these minilateral security partnerships, we have also seen how democracies can stake out strong common positions to uphold regional norms of peace and security, for instance in the context of Chinese revisionism in the South China Sea, where not only leading ASEAN democracies but also Japan, the US, Australia, and India have weighed in on the side of peaceful resolution of disputes and against unilateral use of force or pressure to change the status quo.[9]

DEEPENING TRADE AND INVESTMENT

The business of Asia is business; multinational company spreadsheets do not distinguish between profits earned in authoritarian countries

---

[9] Keck, Zachary. "India Rebukes China on South China Sea," *The Diplomat*, 12 October 2013, http://thediplomat.com/flashpoints-blog/2013/10/12/india-rebukes-beijing-on-south-china-sea/.

and those earned in democracies. But, as Japan learned when its top trading partner in 2010 embargoed the export of rare-earth mineral elements on which Japanese industry relied following a maritime incident at sea, geopolitical rivalries can trump economic cooperation. American corporate leaders used to be the strongest proponents of close and unfettered engagement between the US and China. More recently, many of them have become much harder-nosed about issues like Chinese currency manipulation, pervasive commercial espionage, and the disproportionate role of Chinese state-owned enterprises in a domestic playing field heavily tilted in their favour by virtue of government favouritism and access at non-market rates to real estate, natural resources, and labour.

This is not to uniquely criticise the Chinese model of state capitalism. Rather, it is to highlight that the nature of the political regime in Beijing significantly affects the ability to do business with China. We are seeing this beyond simply the Chinese domestic market: European nations are considering setting up a version of the Committee on Foreign Investment in the United States (CFIUS) to assess the national security implications of direct Chinese investment in sensitive European sectors like telecommunications. India has imposed a host of restrictions on Chinese domestic investment in sensitive sectors, as well as on the role of Chinese workers in Chinese investment projects in India, as a result of national security concerns. The US government has blocked Chinese direct investments in several American sectors, including telecommunications and energy. One reason Myanmar's generals decided to open up their country and re-engage with the West was their understandable fear that China's heavy investments in Myanmar, as well as an influx of Chinese workers, were creating acute political vulnerabilities. When was the last time one heard similar concerns about the political consequences of trade and investment emanating from Australia, Japan, or India?

Rather than universal trade liberalisation through the World Trade Organization, we are seeing the development of a new trend in trade policy: Campaigns for deep regional liberalistion among like-minded and mainly democratic states. These include the Transatlantic Trade and Investment Partnership and the Trans-Pacific Partnership. Precursors to both were the trade negotiations among the North American democracies which produced North American Free Trade Agreement (NAFTA) two decades ago and the construction of the European Common Market among that continent's democracies from the 1950s. All of these agreements among democracies are of a depth and quality that trade agreements struck by authoritarian powers like China and Russia cannot match, in part because of insufficient transparency, trust, and dispute resolution mechanisms resulting from the nature of their political regimes. Russia's blackmailing of Ukraine to reject an economic association agreement with the European Union is a recent, and negative, example of how authoritarian powers wield economic clout to deter political liberalisation in their perceived sphere of influence.

IMPLICATIONS

Some of these initiatives among democratic like-minded nations in Asia will bear fruit; others may fall by the wayside. What is noteworthy is the degree to which Asian powers have leveraged shared values to enhance strategic cooperation around shared interests. The goal is not to contain China or divide Asia into blocs, but to strengthen ties that keep each other and the US committed to a healthy balance of power in Asia, alongside a concomitant balance of influence that privileges democratic norms of transparency, legitimacy, and peaceful cooperation.

There is compelling evidence that, as economic growth increases national capabilities and aspirations in ways that cause their foreign policy horizons to expand, states like Japan, India, and Indonesia are increasingly externalising in their foreign policies elements of their domestic identities as democracies. This effect is accentuated by the shifting power balances and identity dynamics associated with an authoritarian China's rise. In a region divided by Cold War legacies, different degrees of state formation, and disputes over territory and historical memory, a shared belief in good governance and individual rights provides a transnational identity that creates a promising basis for regional cooperation.

None of these developments are directed at China or designed to diminish its security. On the contrary, rather than precluding or undermining Asian democracies' development of constructive relations with China, mutual cooperation to strengthen regional peace and security hedges against the rise of a new hegemonic order, allowing Asian states to engage more confidently with China as a regional partner. China is far more likely to rise peacefully if it can do so in a regional environment anchored by strong market democracies that cooperate deeply among themselves, and with the US, to sustain a liberal order. China can never be master of Asia as long as its vision of authoritarian Sinocentricity threatens the peace and prosperity that have allowed more people in Asia than in any other region of the world to be free.

Daniel Twining is Senior Fellow for Asia at the German Marshall Fund of the United States, where he leads a 16-member team working on the rise of Asia and its implications for the West.

CHAPTER 4

Maritime Multilateral Security Cooperation in East and South Asia

Bonji Ohara

The main issues of maritime security are in the area of security of sea lanes and protection of marine resources.

Insistence on control in enclosed seas or half enclosed seas which have marine resources lends itself to use of drastic measures. In turn, the resulting interference in marine transportation causes serious damage to neighbour countries; even if they are not directly related to underlying resource disputes.

Seaborne transportation is still the dominant mode of transportation used in trade, because ships can carry large cargos across long distances without crossing borders. For example, the sea lane from the Middle East to East China Sea that passes through the Indian Ocean, Malacca Strait and South China Sea (SCS) can be disturbed by territorial disputes between countries.

The threats to sea lanes are not only maritime threats. Others include natural disasters, shipwrecks and piracy. These threats cannot be solved by a single country; multilateral cooperation is needed to treat the threats and to secure safe navigation.

In the 1990s, multilateral security cooperation in Asia expanded both geographically and substantially, to include efforts to build track two consultations among Japan, the US and South Korea. At the same time, however, cooperation over that period also demonstrated major limitations. As a result, Japan and the US came to the conclusion during this period that the ASEAN Regional Forum (ARF) is not a sufficient security framework for Asia, but rather a minor supplement or tool of the Japan–US alliance. This paper demonstrates the limitations of the multilateral security framework in Asia by following its development, and suggesting how to make it more effective.

DEVELOPMENT OF MULTILATERAL SECURITY COOPERATION

Multilateral security cooperation was not only born out of a need for security. The idea of multilateral security cooperation was apparent in the work of the League of Nations following World War I. The Covenant of the League of Nations prohibited war and systemised collective security in which participating nations imposed sanctions jointly against aggressor nations. The security system of the League of Nations, however, failed to prevent World War II because it entrusted the designation of war and sanctions to each nation. The provisions concerning imposition of military sanctions were not binding.

To address this fault, the United Nations (UN) tried to build a powerful and centralised security system by establishing the Security Council which consisted of the five nations which were part of the World War II. Under the UN regime, the Security Council designates the war, and its resolution binds all member nations. This was intended to protect international security. But the divisions of the Cold War contributed to a situation where permanent members of the Security Council so liberally exercised their veto power that they prevented the United Nations Security Council from working. This situation demonstrates the difficulty in translating threat perception into multilateral action.

International society started to appreciate the need for security systems which were not based on the UN. One is non-UN organised peace keeping operations (PKO) and the other is regional or sub-regional security systems. PKO is characterised by third parties providing forces to intervene in disputes by sending disengagement observers or monitoring forces with the agreement of disputing parties and host nations. On the other hand, regional or sub-regional security systems seek to avoid the clash by disputing parties in the first place. Conference on Security and Cooperation in Europe (CSCE) is a successful example of this.

The idea of 'common security' was displayed in the report of Palme Commission in 1982 as follows: 'There can be no hope for victory in a nuclear war; the two sides would be united in suffering and destruction. They can survive only together. They must achieve security not against the adversary but together with him. International security must rest on a commitment to joint survival rather than on a threat of mutual destruction.' This means that shared perceptions are necessary for 'cooperating with enemy'. The ARF was sometimes considered to be an Asian version of CSCE, especially as the CSCE process changed after the Cold War.

THE EFFORT OF BUILDING SECURITY SYSTEM IN ASIA

The ARF was built through Association of Southeast Asian Nations (ASEAN) initiative and was the effort of Asia-Pacific nations broadly. Several Asia-Pacific nations outside of ASEAN had previously proposed building a regional or sub-regional security system.

The Soviet Union was the first nation which proposed to build a security framework in Asia-Pacific region. Former Soviet premiers

Leonid Brezhnev in 1960s and Mikhail Gorbachev in 1980s proposed the 'Asian Collective Security Proposal'. This proposal was refused by Japan and the US because it would have split the Western Bloc, and by China because it appeared to encircle it. In 1990, Australia and Canada tabled a regional security proposal modeled on CSCE. But Japan, the US and China recognised that applying it to Asia was improper because of the differences in Asian and European historical experiences and the specific nature of their security problems.

These proposals, however, presented opportunities for Japan and ASEAN governments to consider a formal regional security system in Asia. The Japanese came up with the idea of developing regional security talks outside the framework of ASEAN talks from the 1970s.

ASEAN countries did not accept the Japanese idea at that time, but 'Singapore Declaration of 1992' said 'ASEAN should intensify its external dialogues in political and security matters by using the ASEAN Post-Ministerial Conferences (PMC),' and the framework for security dialogue was picked up as theme in ASEAN ministerial meeting in July 1992. The Senior Officials Meeting (SOM) for the 1993 ASEAN foreign ministers meeting named it the ASEAN Regional Forum (ARF) and designated member nations.

THE DEVELOPMENT OF MULTILATERAL SECURITY COOPERATION BY ARF

The 'Chairman's Statement' of the first meeting of ARF held in July 1994 said, 'the ARF had enabled the countries in the Asia-Pacific region to foster the habit of constructive dialogue and consultation on political and security issues of common interest and concern. In this respect, the ARF would be in a position to make significant contribution to effort towards confidence-building and preventive diplomacy in the Asia-Pacific region'. It identified 'confidence and security building', 'nuclear non-proliferation', 'peacekeeping cooperation', 'exchanges of non classified military information', 'maritime security', and 'preventive diplomacy' as the subjects of further study.

The Concept Paper of the second meeting of the ARF declared that 'the approach should be taking place in three stages, namely the promotion of confidence building, development of preventive diplomacy, and elaboration of approaches to conflicts.' It said the ARF process is stage one, and should continue to discuss means of implementing confidence building measures (CBM). The second meeting also established track two activities to be carried out by strategic institutes and relevant non-governmental organisations (NGOs). The ARF participants had direct discussions about CBM, PKO, and Search and Rescue in inter-sessional meetings. In the Third Meeting of the ARF, Myanmar and India were approved to join. They also changed the conference pattern from a one-sided Chairman-directed discussion to a discussion guided by Chairman. The ARF that year also showed a positive attitude toward maritime security issues by discussing the SCS.

But in the Fourth Meeting of ARF held in July 1997, although they discussed many problems, including the SCS dispute and the Chairman's statement said 'the process has progressed at a pace acceptable to all participants,' it was apparent that the ARF could not easily move the process forward. Repeated clashes over control of features and EEZs in the SCS testified that multilateral security cooperation in this area would not suffice.

THE LIMITATIONS OF ARF

The ARF is a security system based on multilateral cooperation that includes parties to various disputes, such as in the SCS. It has a structure similar to CSCE. But it is very difficult for members to share threat perceptions, because the scale of territory, population, military force and economy are quite asymmetric between China and ASEAN countries.

The Chinese Navy went into Spratly Islands in 1988 and engaged in an artillery battle with Vietnam Navy, with the result that two Vietnamese ships were sunk and 80 Vietnamese soldiers killed. Although China later promulgated its 'Law on the Territorial Sea' in which it declared sovereignty over the Spratly Islands, Chinese diplomats also declared that China would not cause trouble in a workshop on the South China Sea dispute. The Chinese Navy also posted a territorial marker on Gaven Reef. China's deeds do not match its words, and this inconsistency causes ASEAN countries to be distrustful of China. China's behaviour, however, has not been affected by the distrust and the protests of ASEAN.

China does not recognise ASEAN countries as threats. This asymmetric perception of threat is different from CSCE. The threat which West and East blocs shared was mass destruction by nuclear weapons, and both blocs had the capability to contribute to that outcome. There was a possibility that mutual nuclear attack, which both blocs did not want, would occur. On the contrary, China and ASEAN countries do not share the perception of the common threat. China's negative behavior in the ARF testified to this. China changed its behaviour and tried to concern itself with the ARF positively in 1996. But the change in China's behaviour did not indicate a change in China's perception of threat.

China prefers bilateral talks to multilateral talks for discussions of the dispute in South China Sea because it recognises that multilateral talks will result in it losing advantage over individual ASEAN countries. On the other hand, the problems it creates for multilateral security cooperation isolates China in international society. China is showing its positive attitude to the ARF, but at the same time successfully controlling the pace of the CBM process, from exchange of information to inspection/monitoring and regulation. Chinese marine surveillance ships cut the exploration cables of a Vietnamese oil and gas survey ship *Binh Minh 02* 120 nautical miles off the Vietnamese central coast on 26 May 2011. Public protests in Vietnam followed the Vietnam Foreign Ministry's decision to lodge a formal protest with the Chinese embassy over this incident. There were protests in the Philippines as well against Chinese activity in the Spratly Islands. But none of these protests had any impact on China's behaviour. It continued to develop both the organisations and equipment of the Oceanographic Administration and Fisheries Bureau in order to strengthen its 'management' of the SCS.

The cooperative security which the ARF aims to realise is different from the concept of common security which envisions cooperating with adversaries. Once the antagonism becomes apparent among participating parties, it is difficult to treat it within the framework of cooperative security. It is also difficult to share the perception of threat basic to common security. This means that the ARF is not an effective framework for solving the dispute in SCS. There is a regional limitation too. The ARF usually pays attention to the problems in South East Asia area, because it is lead by ASEAN. However, the ARF can function as an effective maritime multilateral security framework only for natural disasters, shipwrecks and crimes on ocean, etc. in South East Asia area.

SECURITY COOPERATION IN EAST AND SOUTH ASIA

As I mentioned above, the ARF cannot realise the common security framework in the South East Asia region. However, neither is there any effective alternative multilateral security framework in the Asian region.

There is no other security framework which has regular meetings by governments in East and South Asia. Each government is studying the framework mainly through the Track II meetings. None of the countries can entrust their national security to multilateral security cooperation. Every country needs the functions of deterrence and reaction. Therefore, they must seek solutions other than multilateral security cooperation. The expansion of armaments is one such solution. And it can be seen in these areas. But it is not the only solution.

Bilateral security cooperation is another solution. Japan is representative of a country which depends on bilateral security cooperation. Japan has only one ally, the US. The Japan–US alliance is at the core of its security. Japan asserts that multilateral security cooperation is a supplement to the Japan–US alliance. Most Japanese cooperation in military technology, education/training and exercises is with the US. The US and South Korea, not just Japan, also puts bilateral security cooperation at the core of its security.

India, a major power in South Asia, recognises that its main threat is from Pakistan. India recognised the insufficiency of its armaments vis-a-vis Pakistan before the Kargil conflict in 1999, and then continued to expand its armaments including its nuclear weapons. However, if one takes a closer look at India's procurement programmes, it is difficult to say India enjoys specific bilateral cooperation in procurement.

Many observers say 'Malabar,' the joint US–India exercises, demonstrates close US–India relations and India's engagement in South China Sea. US–India security cooperation was developed after the Cold War. They formed a strategic partnership in 2003, but it seems that India did not intend to be 'a member of the US side which contains China in South China Sea. If anything, India prefers to avoid excessive US influence in South Asia, and itself, and keeps a certain distance from the US. On the other hand, the defence agreement concerning education and training between India and Vietnam, and their cooperation on joint exploitation of gas and oil in South China Sea, testify to India's strengthening engagement in the South China Sea. This is the reason that China is irritated by India's behaviour.

Security cooperation in South Asia, regardless of whether it is multilateral or bilateral, is not as prominent a feature of the security environment as it is in East Asia. India's principle interest is in trying to maintain its influence in this area.

MARITIME MULTILATERAL SECURITY COOPERATION IN ASIA

Although, under these circumstances it's difficult to build an effective multilateral security cooperation framework, the immediate necessity of maritime multilateral security cooperation in the region is quite compelling.

Multilateral security cooperation framework faces many contradictions in Asia. But there are hints of success in the present environment. There are effective bilateral security cooperation frameworks that can be networked. In this network, every country which has some bilateral cooperation with other countries in the region will be involved in every issue at each level. It can choose the participating parties dependent on the issue and build ad hoc multilateral security cooperation.

Each country in Asia tries to secure the function of deterrence and reaction by strengthening bilateral security cooperation. This is because of difficulties in sharing the perception of threat among all of the participants in the multilateral security cooperation system, particularly in dealing with severe disputes. It is easier to achieve the common perception of threat in the context of bilateral security cooperation. Maritime security will not allow each country to wait for the development of a multilateral security cooperation framework. On the other hand, bilateral security cooperation is not effective enough.

Therefore, each country has to work toward building a network of bilateral security cooperation. Each country has to take concrete measures with a country which shares its threat perception and try to involve other countries by adjusting their interests based on bilateral security cooperation on an issue by issue basis. There has already been success in the development of Japan–South Korea security cooperation based on the Japan–US alliance and US–South Korea alliance.

CONCLUSION

Maritime security requires multilateral cooperation, but there are a wide variety of issues involved. Some of them can be treated by multilateral security frameworks like the ARF, and some cannot. The nature of the seas is such that their security and safety cover vast areas and are connected with other seas. Therefore, maritime security requires the flexible multilateral cooperation of countries across the areas concerned; a permanent framework with fixed participating parties cannot function.

Bilateral cooperation between countries is developing concrete measures against common threats. Multilateral frameworks require consensus before taking action. But in the bilateral framework, two countries with shared threat perception can take action quickly. And if every country has bilateral security cooperation with another, then those countries can cooperate on a multilateral basis issue by issue. They thereby create an ad hoc multilateral security cooperation framework.

Ad hoc multilateral security cooperation based on bilateral security cooperation can be one of the solutions to maritime security in the Asian region, and it can influence the behaviour of countries which threaten security.

The next problem is how to build the perception of 'the common interest' in the Asian region. The countries in the region need reasons to cooperate. If a country can benefit by cooperating with another country, then the country has incentive to cooperate. This kind of incentive will compensate the differences of threat perception among countries. For example, if the countries use the same equipment or system as a 'common asset', it can give them business opportunities, too. It can be one of the 'common interest'. We have to seek the assets which can provide them 'benefit'. And then they can create the layers of cooperative network. The layers of network which lap over the region will make security cooperation more effective.

Bonji Ohara is a Research Fellow and Project Manager specialising in foreign and security policy and China at The Tokyo Foundation.

CHAPTER 5

Maritime Security and the Law of the Sea

SAM BATEMAN

For nearly 350 years from the time of Grotius in the early seventeenth century until the 1950s and 60s, the international law of the sea was largely unchanged and dictated by the major maritime powers. The freedom of the seas was the dominant paradigm with only a narrow belt of territorial sea under the jurisdiction of coastal states. All this changed with the greater number of independent states in the period of de-colonisation following World War II. The influence of these states on the law of the sea is evident in the 1982 UN Convention on the Law of the Sea (UNCLOS), particularly with its introduction of a twelve-mile limit to the territorial sea and the regimes of the Exclusive Economic Zone (EEZ) and archipelagic state.

As Professor RP Anand, an eminent Indian scholar and historian of the law of the sea, aptly observed in 1982, there have been 'more changes and progress in ocean law since 1967 than in the previous

200 years'.[1] Moreover, the pace of evolution of the customary law of the sea has not slowed since 1982. The developments in ocean law over the last thirty years are almost as significant as those that occurred between 1967 and 1982, particularly through increased concern for the health of the world's oceans and a proliferation of international treaties affecting ocean usage. The dominant paradigms during this period have been increased coastal state control over adjacent waters and new limitations on the freedom of the high seas, especially with regard to freedom of fishing.

Coastal states are moving towards increased regulation of their adjacent waters. Greater concern for protection of marine environment largely drives this development although major Asia-Pacific countries, China, India and Japan, also seek increased control due to security concerns. Environmental concerns were behind Australia's introduction of compulsory pilotage in the Torres Strait. The legal justification for this step was questioned by the United States (US) and Singapore.[2] The US was concerned that compulsory pilotage in the Torres Strait might provide a precedent for other straits in the region, notably Hormuz and Malacca.

Perhaps unintentionally, Australia has supported trends towards broader coastal state control of adjacent waters with actions such as the introduction of compulsory pilotage in the Torres Strait, the declaration of prohibited anchorage areas around undersea cables in the EEZ,[3] the introduction of mandatory ship reporting in parts of the EEZ adjacent to the Great Barrier Reef, and the declaration

---

[1] Anand, R.P. *Origin and Development of the Law of the Sea*, The Hague: Martinus Nijhoff, 1982, p.219.

[2] Bateman, Sam. "The Compulsory Pilotage Regime in the Torres Strait – A "Melting Pot" of Operational, Legal and Political Considerations" in *The Future of Ocean Regime Building: Essays in Tribute to Douglas M Johnston*, Aldo Chircop and Ted McDorman (eds), Leiden: Brill/ Martinus Nijhoff Publishers, 2009, pp. 261-286.

[3] *Guide to Australian Maritime Security Arrangements*, Canberra: Australian Border Protection Command, December 2009, Figure 8, p. 30

of the entire Australian EEZ as a submarine exercise area.[4] These developments are despite Australia being normally a strong supporter of freedom of navigation with a particular concern for navigational rights in the archipelagos to its north.

There are important implications here for the international law of the sea and how it might evolve in the future. Where differences are evident at present between Western, primarily American, views of the law of the sea,[5] and those of the rising powers of Asia, there can be no certainty that the Western views will continue to prevail. Unfortunately, UNCLOS has many 'gray areas' and ambiguities that allow opposing views to sit side-by-side. This is particularly the case with military operations in the EEZ.

THE LAW OF THE SEA IN THE ASIA-PACIFIC

Largely as a consequence of the maritime geography of the Asia-Pacific region, particularly in East Asia with its large EEZs, many islands and archipelagos, overlapping claims to maritime jurisdiction, and many strategically important shipping 'choke points', the international law of the sea is of great importance in the region. Indeed, it is difficult to fully appreciate maritime security in the region without some understanding of the law of the sea. Examples of all the contentious issues with the contemporary law of the sea can be found in the region, and these constitute a source of tension and even potential conflict. A key causal factor is the long-standing tension between maritime powers seeking maximum freedoms to use the sea, and coastal states seeking to restrict these freedoms in their adjacent waters. Importantly, the coastal state view is the dominant paradigm in the region.

---

[4] Australian Hydrographic Service, 'Information Concerning Submarines', *Australian Annual Notice to Mariners*, No. 19, para. 3.

[5] These views have been comprehensively described recently in Kraska, James, *Maritime Power and the Law of the Sea – Expeditionary Operations in World Politics*, New York: Oxford University Press, 2011.

A fundamental challenge with regional maritime security is that most regional countries and Western maritime powers differ on key laws of the sea issues. These differences are evident with the use of territorial sea straight baselines,[6] the ability of a warship to transit the territorial sea without providing prior notification to the coastal state,[7] and rights and duties in an EEZ. These differences may be increasing. Thailand, for example, ratified UNCLOS in May 2011, but in doing so, made the following statement:

> The Government of the Kingdom of Thailand understands that, in the exclusive economic zone, enjoyment of the freedom of navigation in accordance with relevant provisions of the Convention excludes any non-peaceful use without the consent of the coastal state, in particular, military exercises or other activities which may affect the rights or interests of the coastal state; and it also excludes the threat or use of force against the territorial integrity, political independence, peace or security of the coastal state. [8]

This declaration is very similar to China's position on military activities in an EEZ. It is understood that the US made strong diplomatic representations to Thailand against such a statement, but Thailand went ahead regardless.

---

[6] Almost all East Asian countries (i.e. Cambodia, China, Japan, North Korea, South Korea, Malaysia, Myanmar, Thailand and Vietnam) have used a straight baseline system—most appear excessive in terms of what is customarily regarded as acceptable under international law. Malaysia and Vietnam implicitly accepted each other's excessive straight baselines in their joint submission to the Commission on the Limits of the Continental Shelf for an extended continental shelf in the South China Sea. Bateman, Sam and Schofield, Clive. "State Practice regarding Straight Baselines in East Asia—Legal, Technical and Political Issues in a Changing Environment", Paper for international conference on 'The Difficulties of Implementing the Provisions of UNCLOS', International Hydrographic Bureau, Monaco, 16-17 October 2008, http://www.gmat.unsw.edu.au/ablos/ ABLOS08Folder/ablos08_papers.htm.

[7] Many coastal states in the Asia-Pacific region have such a requirement, including China, India, Indonesia, South Korea, the Philippines and Vietnam.

[8] United Nations, Statement by Thailand on Ratifying UNCLOS, 25 May 2011, C.N.291.2011. TREATIES-4 (Depositary Notification), http://treaties.un.org/doc/Publication/CN/2011/CN.291.2011-Eng.pdf.

THE LEGAL STATUS OF REGIONAL SEAS

The geographical picture of concavity along the continental coastline of East Asia and the numerous off-lying archipelagos and islands creates a large array of enclosed or semi-enclosed seas, such as the Sea of Japan (or East Sea to the Koreans), East China Sea, South China Sea, Gulf of Thailand, Sulu Sea, and the Timor and Arafura Seas. An enclosed or semi-enclosed sea is defined by UNCLOS Article 122 as 'a gulf, basin or sea surrounded by two or more states and connected to another sea or the ocean by a narrow outlet or consisting entirely or primarily of the territorial seas and exclusive economic zones of two or more coastal states.'

Most regional seas are 'semi-enclosed seas' covered by Part IX of UNCLOS. Use of the words 'should cooperate' and 'shall endeavour' in Article 123 of UNCLOS places a strong obligation on the littoral states to coordinate their activities as defined in the sub-paragraphs of that article. While resource management, the protection of the marine environment and marine scientific research are mentioned specifically as areas for cooperation, the opening sentence of Article 123 creates a more general obligation to cooperate. It is an unfortunate consequence of the sovereignty disputes in the South China Sea that the littoral states are failing to implement their obligation to cooperate.[9]

Semi-enclosed seas are not 'international waters'. Rather, they largely comprise the EEZs of the littoral countries, which have significant rights and duties in the seas, as set out in UNCLOS Part V defining the EEZ regime. The use of the term 'international waters' by the US goes dangerously close to taking the world back to a pre-UNCLOS era when the Western maritime powers argued that the

---

[9] Bateman, Sam. "Sovereignty as an Obstacle to Effective Oceans Governance and Maritime Boundary Making—the Case of the South China Sea" in *Limits of Maritime Jurisdiction*, Clive Schofield, Seokwoo Lee and Moon-Sang Kwon (eds), Leiden: Brill Academic Publishers, 2013, pp. 201-224.

extended offshore resources zone (which became the EEZ) should be an extension of the high seas while coastal states tended to see it as an extended territorial sea. The solution was an EEZ that is *sui generis*, i.e. a zone all of its own, neither high seas nor territorial sea, subject in accordance with UNCLOS Article 55 to its own specific legal regime. Use of the term 'international waters' derogates from the agreed nature of the EEZ.

The US includes EEZs within its operational definition of 'international waters' because, in accordance with UNCLOS Article 58(1), other states have the freedoms of navigation and overflight in the EEZ of a coastal state, as well as the freedom to lay submarine cables and pipelines, and other internationally lawful uses of the sea related to those freedoms. However, UNCLOS Article 58(3) requires that, in exercising these freedoms, other states should have due regard to the rights and duties of the coastal state. In practice, however, it is proving very difficult to define an operational test to distinguish between an action that has due regard to the rights and duties of the other party, and one that does not.

MILITARY ACTIVITIES IN AN EEZ

Several clashes have occurred in the East Asian seas between American and Chinese vessels and aircraft. The US argues that its military activities in China's EEZ are an exercise of the freedoms of navigation and overflight, while China argues that some of these activities do not have due regard to its rights in its EEZ, such as its jurisdiction over marine scientific research. Other states, including India, Malaysia and Thailand, appear to share China's view. As virtually all East Asian maritime space is the claimed EEZ of one country or another, these fundamental differences over rights and duties in an EEZ have significant implications for building maritime security in the region.

Two issues lie at the heart of this problem. The first is interpreting what activities by a coastal state do not have 'due regard' to the rights and duties of another state in its EEZ,[10] and, similarly, what activities by other states in an EEZ do not have 'due regard' to the rights of the coastal state.[11] However, there is a considerable range of opinions regarding the meaning of 'due regard' and what precisely are the 'rights and duties' of the separate states. The basic principles should be that states engaging in military activities should not unreasonably interfere with coastal state rights to explore and exploit the natural resources of the EEZ, or with its duties to preserve and protect the marine environment and manage the living resources of the EEZ.

Due to the way in which UNCLOS was negotiated by consensus and the differences of view over the status of the EEZ mentioned earlier, as well as a failure to define key terms in the convention, it does not provide clear guidance on these issues. It is well accepted now that the high seas navigational and overflight freedoms available in an EEZ under UNCLOS Articles 58 and 87 are not absolute. They must be conducted with 'due regard' to the rights and duties of the coastal state. Hence, military activities conducted in a marine protected area legitimately declared by a coastal state in its EEZ, or an area of known high fishing activity would contravene this principle.

The second issue is interpreting what constitutes marine scientific research, which is under the jurisdiction of a coastal state in its EEZ,[12] and what does not. UNCLOS Article 56(b)(ii) provides that the coastal state has jurisdiction over marine scientific research in its EEZ. However, UNCLOS does not define the key terms 'marine scientific research', 'survey activities', 'hydrographic survey' or 'military survey'. Maritime powers believe that 'survey activities' are not marine scientific research and point out that UNCLOS distinguishes between 'research' and 'marine scientific research' on the

---

[10] In accordance with UNCLOS Article 56(2).

[11] In accordance with UNCLOS Article 58(3).

[12] Article 56(1)(b)(ii) of UNCLOS.

one hand, and 'hydrographic surveys' and 'survey activities' on the other, primarily because these are sometimes referred to separately in the Convention, although this is a questionable argument.[13] While the coastal state might regulate marine scientific research in its EEZ and on its continental shelf, the US believes that hydrographic and military survey activities are freedoms that the coastal state cannot regulate in its EEZ. They are freedoms captured by the expressions 'other internationally lawful uses of the sea' related to freedoms of navigation and overflight in article 58(1) of UNCLOS and inter alia in Article 87(1) of the convention.

I have argued elsewhere that due to advances in technology and the increased utility of hydrographic surveys, these surveys should be subject to marine scientific research regime in UNCLOS Part XIII and under the jurisdiction of a coastal state in its EEZ.[14] The United States equates 'military surveys' with 'hydrographic surveys', but this seems unwise.[15] The term 'military data gathering' used by the United Kingdom (UK) is preferable because it associates the activity with the general right to conduct military activities in the EEZ of another state rather than with the questionable right to conduct hydrographic surveys in the EEZ without coastal state notice or consent. The argument that data collection purely for military purposes is a freedom of navigation available in an EEZ has more strength than the argument that hydrographic surveys can be conducted in an EEZ without the consent of the coastal state.

---

[13] Bateman, Sam. "A Response to Pedrozo – The Wider Utility of Hydrographic Surveys", *Chinese Journal of International Law*, No. 10, 2011, doi: 10.1093/chinesejil/jmq036, paras 7-8.

[14] Ibid.

[15] An earlier discussion of issues arising from the conduct of hydrographic surveying in an EEZ may be found in Bateman, Sam, "Hydrographic Surveying in Exclusive Economic Zones: Jurisdictional Issues", 5 *International Hydrographic Review (New Series)* (2004), pp. 24-33; and Bateman, Sam, "Hydrographic Surveying in the EEZ: Differences and Overlaps with Marine Scientific Research", 29 *Marine Policy* (2005), pp. 163-174.

In an attempt to clarify these issues and to provide a regional maritime confidence and security building measure, the Ocean Policy Research Foundation (OPRF) of Japan developed 'Guidelines for Navigation and Overflight in the Exclusive Economic Zone'.[16] These set out broad principles of common understanding regarding certain aspects of navigation and overflight in the EEZ, including military and intelligence gathering activities. Unfortunately, an American position has been that these guidelines are 'unacceptable even as a starting point'.[17] Most recently, the OPRF has developed a simpler document, 'Principles for Building Confidence and Security in the Exclusive Economic Zones of the Asia-Pacific' with the aim of overcoming the objections to the earlier guidelines. These principles accept that military activities in an EEZ are legitimate, subject to having due regard to the rights of the coastal state, and identify activities that would not have such regard.

CONCLUSION

Differences of view regarding key law of the sea issues are a fundamental problem of maritime security in the Asia-Pacific region. Regional recognition of the OPRF's non-binding principles would assist in alleviating this problem. The situation is not helped, however, by the US remaining outside UNCLOS. As was demonstrated by Thailand's statement regarding military activities in the EEZ despite representations from Washington, the US lacks credibility on the law of the sea while it is not a party to the convention. This places a significant limitation on the ability of the US to play the leadership role in regional maritime security that regional countries expect it to play.

---

[16] The Guidelines are available online at: http://www.sof.or.jp/topics/2005_e/pdf/20051205_e. pdf.

[17] Pedrozo, Raul (Pete). "Preserving Navigational Rights and Freedoms: The Right to Conduct Military Activities in China's Exclusive Economic Zone", *Chinese Journal of International Law*, No. 9, 2010, pp. 9-29.

Sam Bateman is Adviser to the Maritime Security Programme at the S Rajaratnam School of International Studies (RSIS), Nanyang Technological University, Singapore.

CHAPTER 6

A National Strategy for the South China Sea

Steven Groves

The status quo in the South China Sea (SCS) is unsustainable. Over the past several years, China has aggressively pursued its 'nine-dash line' claim of sovereignty over all land features in the SCS and its assertion of 'sovereign rights and jurisdiction' over all of the waters lying within the nine-dash line. In a throwback to the days of John Selden's *Mare Clausum*, China has essentially claimed the entirety of the SCS as its Exclusive Economic Zone (EEZ).

Attempts to peacefully resolve sovereignty and maritime disputes in the SCS have been boycotted by China or have stalled. China has refused to arbitrate with the Philippines regarding the meaning of its nine-dash line, and efforts to formalise the Declaration on the Conduct of Parties in the SCS into a binding code of conduct have thus far been unsuccessful.

China has taken its wildly excessive claim beyond the realm of theory, harassing fishing and oil exploration vessels and of Vietnam and the Philippines in recent years. Most alarmingly, China has confronted, harassed, and attempted to damage US military survey vessels acting lawfully within the SCS. In what may be a prelude to future Chinese acts in the SCS, China declared an Air Defence Identification Zone in the East China Sea that includes the airspace of the disputed Senkaku Islands.

The US must confront this aggression by developing and promulgating a National Strategy for the South China Sea (NSSCS), declaring the US red lines in the SCS and making clear that the US will protect its national interests in the region.

While China will certainly protest the release of a US national strategy document, it is hardly in a position to complain due to the historically excessive claim it has made to sovereignty over the entire SCS.

CHINA'S *MARE CLAUSUM*

More than 800 years ago, Pope Alexander III granted sovereignty over the entire Adriatic Sea to the city state of Venice. In a ceremony that began in 1176 and was repeated annually, the Pope presented the Doge of Venice with a golden ring which he would cast into the Adriatic, symbolically marrying Venice to the sea. Even though Venice did not possess both shores of the Adriatic, it enforced its jurisdiction over the sea through the use of force.[1]

Three hundred years later, papal sanction was again sought regarding sovereignty over the entire Atlantic Ocean. To resolve disputes and avoid conflict between maritime powers Spain and Portugal, in 1493 Pope Alexander VI issued a bull dividing the Atlantic Ocean from pole to pole, granting Spain sovereignty over all lands to the west of the line and Portugal everything to the east. The papal grant included a monopoly over all commerce within the divided areas 'so that other nations could not trade without

---

[1] Theutenberg, Bo Johnson. "Mare Clausum et Mare Liberum," *Arctic*, Vol. 37, No. 4 (1984), p. 481, 488-89, http://arctic.synergiesprairies.ca/arctic/index.php/arctic/article/view/2230.

license from the Spanish or Portuguese sovereign.' Navigation and trade within the Atlantic without a royal license was punishable by death.[2]

A century later in 1609, the debate over whether maritime states could exercise sovereign rights to such vast bodies of water came to a head with the publication of Hugo Grotius' *Mare Liberum* ('free sea'). Grotius' famous essay was 'an earnest and powerful appeal... made to the civilised world for complete freedom of the high seas for the innocent use and mutual benefit of all.' Grotius declared that the Spanish and Portuguese claims and the papal bulls that granted them were invalid under the 'law of nations.'[3] According to Grotius, the sea is *res nullius* ('nobody's property') and as the 'common property of all...no one may be lawfully barred from travelling across it.'[4]

The Stuart kings of Great Britain, desiring to retain exclusive fishing rights in waters to their north and west, responded by publishing John Selden's *Mare Clausum* ('enclosed sea') in 1635. But the position argued by Selden 'was moribund, opposed to the growing spirit of freedom throughout the world and to the emerging principle of *mare liberum*.' Grotius' view regarding dominion over the seas prevailed:

> The Law of Nations developed along the lines proposed by Grotius. More and more, the principle was recognised that the high seas should be open and free for the use of all nations. No nation could prevent another from carrying on traditional activities at sea. The exclusive sovereign claims over vast areas of the sea had to be abandoned.[5]

---

[2] Theutenberg, Bo Johnson. "Mare Clausum et Mare Liberum," p. 490.

[3] *Ibid.*, at p. 491.

[4] Vieira, Monica Brito. "Mare Liberum vs. Mare Clausum: Grotius, Freitas, and Selden's Debate on Dominion over the Seas," *Journal of the History of Ideas*, Vol. 64, No. 3 (July 2003), p. 370.

[5] Theutenberg, Bo Johnson. "Mare Clausum et Mare Liberum," p. 492.

Centuries have passed since the Grotian view was accepted that no nation may claim sovereignty over the world's oceans, with the exception of a narrow band of water extending from the nation's coast known as the 'territorial sea.' By the early nineteenth century it was 'almost universally accepted' that the breadth of the territorial sea was three nautical miles and that any waters seaward of that limit were open to navigation by all nations.[6]

In 2009, four hundred years after the publication of *Mare Liberum*, the Chinese government claimed jurisdiction and control over the entire South China Sea. On 6 May 2009, Malaysia and Vietnam made a joint submission to the Commission on the Limits of the Continental Shelf regarding the outer limits of their respective continental shelves.[7] The next day, China sent a letter to the UN Secretary-General objecting to the Malaysia–Vietnam submission, calling it a serious infringement upon 'China's sovereignty, sovereign rights and jurisdiction in the South China Sea.'[8]

Accompanying China's letter was a map of the SCS, bound by a U-shaped, nine-dash line that begins off the coast of Vietnam, moves south until it reaches a point off the coast of Malaysia, and then travels north-east to the Philippines, ending off the east coast of Taiwan. (Compare Appendix A and B, illustrating the vast difference between China's actual EEZ and its nine-dash line claim).

In regard to the status of the area depicted within the nine-dash line, China's letter states:

---

[6]Koh, Tommy TB. "Negotiating a New World Order for the Sea," *Virginia Journal of International Law*, Vol. 24, No. 4 (1984), pp. 762-763.

[7]Joint submission by Malaysia and the Socialist Republic of Vietnam to the Commission on the Limits of the Continental Shelf, http://www.un.org/Depts/los/clcs_new/submissions_files/submission_mysvnm_33_2009.htm.

[8]Communication from the Permanent Mission of the People's Republic of China to the United Nations, 7 May 2009, http://www.un.org/Depts/los/clcs_new/submissions_files/mysvnm33_09/chn_2009re_mys_vnm_e.pdf.

China has indisputable sovereignty over the islands in the South China Sea and the adjacent waters, and enjoys sovereign rights and jurisdiction over the relevant waters as well as the seabed and subsoil thereof (see attached map).

While China has never clarified the precise basis or legal status of its nine-dash line claims, the language China uses in its letter is similar to the text of Article 56 of the UN Convention on the Law of the Sea: 'Rights, jurisdiction and duties of the coastal State in the exclusive economic zone.' Pursuant to Article 56(a), a coastal state has 'sovereign rights' in its EEZ to exploit the living and non-living natural resources in the water and on the seabed.[9] Under Article 56(b) a coastal state has 'jurisdiction' with regard to establishing artificial islands, conducting marine scientific research, and protecting the marine environment.[10]

As such, a fair reading of the nine-dash line letter is that China: (1) claims sovereignty over all islands within the nine-dash line (e.g. the Spratly and Paracel island groups) and their adjacent waters (i.e. their respective territorial seas), and (2) declares 'sovereign rights and jurisdiction' over the 'relevant waters' (i.e. the waters seaward of the territorial sea, such as the EEZ) as well as the seabed extending from the islands.

CHINA'S CLAIMS VIOLATE THE LAW OF THE SEA
The UN Convention on the Law of the Sea (UNCLOS) makes it clear that all nations have the right to navigate their warships on and

---

[9]UNCLOS, Art. 56(1)(a), and Wilson, Brian, "An Avoidable Maritime Conflict: Disputes Regarding Military Activities in the Exclusive Economic Zone," *Journal of Maritime Law & Commerce*, Vol. 41, No. 3 (July 2010), p. 423, http://papers.ssrn.com/sol3/papers. cfm?abstract_id=2019465. Coastal states also have sovereign rights "with regard to other activities for the economic exploitation and exploration of the zone, such as the production of energy from the water, currents and winds".

[10]UNCLOS, Art. 56(1)(b). Article 56 also contains a residual clause stating that a coastal state has "other rights and duties" in its EEZ as "provided for in the convention."

their aircraft over the EEZ of a foreign nation so long as those ships and aircraft do not exploit the natural resources of the foreign EEZ. While military survey activities are considered prejudicial to the peace and security of a coastal state if conducted within its twelve nm territorial sea, nothing in UNCLOS prohibits such activities outside of the territorial sea.[11]

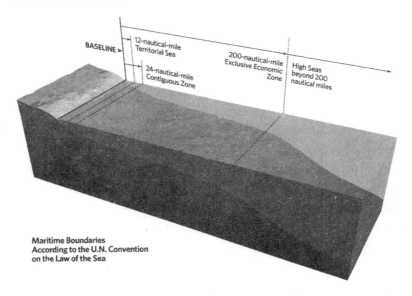

BASELINE ➤

12-nautical-mile Territorial Sea

24-nautical-mile Contiguous Zone

200-nautical-mile Exclusive Economic Zone

High Seas beyond 200 nautical miles

Maritime Boundaries
According to the U.N. Convention
on the Law of the Sea

China seeks to extend the prohibition on military surveys to its EEZ.[12] But Part V of UNCLOS (titled 'Exclusive Economic Zone') is clear that restrictions regarding activities within the EEZ relate solely to economic matters and are not military in nature.

Moreover, Article 87 of UNCLOS is titled 'Freedom of the high seas' and is located in Part VII (titled 'High Seas'). That article lists the rights of all states while operating on the high seas, including, inter alia: (a) freedom of navigation (b) freedom of overflight

---

[11]UNCLOS, Art. 19(2)(j).

[12]See Order of the President No. 75, "Surveying and Mapping Law of the People's Republic of China," 29 August 2002, http://english.gov.cn/laws/2005-10/09/content_75314.htm.

(c) freedom to lay submarine cables and pipelines (d) freedom to construct artificial islands and other installations permitted under international law (e) freedom of fishing, and (f) freedom of scientific research.[13]

The rights and duties of other states operating within the EEZ of a coastal state are also set forth in Part V. In particular, article 58 (titled 'Rights and duties of other States in the exclusive economic zone') makes it clear that all states may exercise broad high seas freedoms while operating within a foreign EEZ. Specifically, it says that all states 'enjoy, subject to the relevant provisions of this Convention, the freedoms referred to in Article 87 of navigation and overflight' within the EEZ of a coastal state, thereby incorporating by reference all of the navigational rights and freedoms listed in Article 87.

Article 58 goes further to make clear that high seas freedoms shall be enjoyed by vessels operating within a foreign EEZ by explicitly referencing the rest of Part VII's navigational provisions: 'Articles 88 to 115 and other pertinent rules of international law apply to the exclusive economic zone in so far as they are not incompatible with this Part.' Articles 88 to 115 set forth the general provisions applicable to the high seas, and include the right of navigation (Article 90), immunity of warships from the jurisdiction of any other state (Article 95), and the right to seize a pirate ship or aircraft (Article 105).

As such, the plain language of UNCLOS is explicit: All states enjoy the freedom of navigation and overflight while operating within a foreign EEZ.

CHINA'S AGGRESSIVE DEFENCE OF
ITS EXCESSIVE CLAIMS

China has not sat idly by in regard to its excessive maritime claims, but rather has taken aggressive measures to enforce them. China has a history of resorting to violence in connection with its SCS

---

[13] UNCLOS, Art. 87(1).

claims, seizing the Western Paracels from Vietnam in 1974, sinking three Vietnamese vessels in 1988, and taking Mischief Reef from the Philippines in 1995.

China's propensity for confrontation and violence has continued in recent years. Since 2009 the US, Vietnam, and the Philippines have been repeatedly harassed in the SCS while engaging in lawful activities. Chinese patrol boats and military vessels have on a regular basis confronted, challenged, and sometimes perpetrated acts of violence against US military survey vessels as well as Philippine and Vietnamese fishing boats and commercial survey vessels.

AMONG THE MORE NOTABLE RECENT INCIDENTS:

- 8 March 2009: Five Chinese vessels harassed the USNS *Impeccable* while it was engaging in lawful military surveillance activities in the SCS approximately 75 miles from Chinese territory. The vessels threatened to collide with the unarmed *Impeccable* on several occasions and attempted to destroy its towed sonar array.[14]

- 11 June 2009: A Chinese submarine 'inadvertently' struck and damaged the sonar array being towed by the USS *John S McCain*, an Arleigh Burke-class destroyer operating in the SCS approximately 144 miles outside of Subic Bay.[15]

- 25 February 2011: A Chinese frigate fired three shots at Philippine fishing vessel *F/V Maricris 12* in Jackson Atoll.[16]

[14] Odom, Jonathan. "The True 'Lies' of the Impeccable Incident: What Really Happened, Who Disregarded International Law, and Why Every Nation (Outside of China) Should Be Concerned," *Michigan State Journal of International Law*, Vol. 3, Issue 18 (2010), http://papers.ssrn.com/sol3/papers.cfm?abstract_id=1622943.

[15] Carter, David and Slavin, Erik. "USS McCain arrives at Sasebo after suffering damage to sonar array," *Stars and Stripes*, 17 June 2009, http://www.stripes.com/news/uss-mccain-arrives-at-sasebo-after-suffering-damage-to-sonar-array-1.92521.

[16] Jamandre, Tessa. "China fired at Filipino fishermen in Jackson atoll," *ABS-CBN News*, 3 June 2011, http://www.abs-cbnnews.com/-depth/06/02/11/china-fired-filipino-fishermen-jackson-atoll.

- 2 March 2011: A seismic survey vessel *M/V Veritas Voyager* leased by the Philippines was harassed in Reed Bank by two Chinese patrol boats.[17]
- 21-25 May 2011: According to the Philippines, Chinese vessels unloaded construction materials (steel posts) and placed a buoy near Amy Douglas Bank, which is considered to show an intention by China to build a structure and block off the area.[18]
- 26 May 2011: Chinese patrol boats deliberately cut a submerged cable of the *Binh Minh 02* oil and gas survey ship operated by PetroVietnam while operating in Vietnamese waters, 80 miles off of the south-central coast of Vietnam. China stated that the operations 'undermined China's interests and jurisdictional rights.'[19]
- 8 June 2011: A Chinese vessel used 'specialised cable-cutting equipment' to intentionally damage the seismic exploration cables of the *Viking 2* while it was exploring for oil under contract with PetroVietnam.[20]
- 5 July 2011: Chinese soldiers boarded a Vietnamese fishing boat near the Paracel Islands in disputed waters, punched

---

[17] "China and the Philippines: Implications of the Reed Bank Incident," *Jamestown Foundation*, China Brief, Volume 11, Issue 8, 6 May 2011, http://www.jamestown.org/single/?no_cache=1&tx_ttnews%5Btt_news%5D=37902&tx_ttnews%5BbackPid%5D=517#. UmBCKPmsh8E, and Peter A Dutton, "The Sino–Philippine Row: International Arbitration and the South China Sea".

[18] Banlaoi, Rommel C. "A Mischief Reef in the Making?", *Declassified Information*, 3 June 2011, http://declassifiedrommelbanlaoi.blogspot.com/2011/06/mischief-reef-in-making.html.

[19] "Chinese marine surveillance ships violate Vietnam's sovereignty," *The Voice of Vietnam Online*, 28 May 2011, http://english.vov.vn/Politics/Chinese-marine-surveillance-ships-violate-Vietnams-sovereignty/225186.vov, and "Vietnam accuses China in seas dispute," *BBC News*, 30 May 2011, http://www.bbc.co.uk/news/world-asia-pacific-13592508.

[20] "Vietnam's vessel Viking 2 'harassed' many times," *Vietnamnet Bridge*, 10 June 2011, http://english.vietnamnet.vn/fms/government/8963/vietnam-s-vessel-viking-2--harassed--many-times.html.

and kicked its captain, threatened other crew members, and confiscated one tonne of fish.[21]

- 3 March 2012: China detained and held twenty-one Vietnamese fishermen near the Paracel Islands for seven weeks.[22]
- 8 April 2012: Beginning of standoff between Philippine and Chinese ships at Scarborough Shoal after a Philippine Navy ship boarded Chinese fishing vessels and found sharks, corrals and giant clams.[23]
- 30 November 2012: Chinese fishing vessels cut the survey cables of the *Binh Minh 02* for a second time, this time just outside of the Gulf of Tonkin.[24]

By slowly but steadily using these tactics to ratchet up the pressure on its smaller SCS neighbours, China has achieved de facto sovereignty over various disputed land features.

The ramifications for the US interests are significant. The official position of the US is that it does not take a position on the issue of sovereignty over the various SCS land features. But China's steady acquisition of such features in the past and its clear intent to acquire additional features in the future affects the US interests in the SCS due to the fact that such acquisitions serve as the basis for China's excessive maritime claims.

---

[21]"Vietnam: Chinese soldiers attack fishermen," *Associated Press*, 14 July 2011, http://news.yahoo.com/vietnam-chinese-soldiers-attack-fishermen-052853883.html.

[22]"China frees Vietnamese fishermen held on Paracel Islands," *BBC News (Asia)*, 21 April 2012, http://www.bbc.co.uk/news/world-asia-17796451.

[23]Jane Perlez, "Philippines and China Ease Tensions in Rift at Sea, *The New York Times*, 18 June 2012, http://www.nytimes.com/2012/06/19/world/asia/beijing-and-manila-ease-tensions-in-south-china-sea.html.

[24]"PetroVietnam protests Chinese ships' cutting of survey cable," *People's Army Newspaper Online*, 4 December 2012, http://www.qdnd.vn/qdndsite/en-US/75/72/306/306/306/218761/Default.aspx, and "PetroVietnam Protests Chinese Ships' Breakage of Survey Cable," *Bien Gioi Lanh Tho*, 13 December 2012, http://biengioilanhtho.gov.vn/eng/petrovietnamprotestschineseships-breakageof-nd-4466f14c.aspx.

Each SCS atoll or coral reef acquired by China provides it with an additional land feature from which to claim—validly or invalidly—a territorial sea and an EEZ. In turn, each territorial sea and EEZ thus acquired by China further justifies its nine-dash line claim and strengthens its protests against the US military activities in the SCS waters surrounding the acquired land features.

As such, the US does itself a disservice by continuing to pretend that it does not have a stake in the outcome of sovereignty disputes over SCS land features. It is time that the US amend its policy of neutrality in this regard.

ATTEMPTS TO RESOLVE SCS DISPUTES PEACEFULLY HAVE FAILED

Releasing a National Strategy document is a peaceful, but forceful way for the US to make clear to China that the US places a high priority on protecting its national interests in the SCS. Forcefulness, rather than continuing the status quo, is required at this point in time due to China's proven belligerence and its general reluctance to resolve SCS disputes in a peaceful manner.

The nations bordering the SCS, including China, have ostensibly pledged to settle their SCS disputes in a peaceful manner—a pledge that has been repeatedly broken by China. More than a decade ago, on 4 November 2002, China and all ten ASEAN nations signed the Declaration on the Conduct of Parties in the South China Sea (DoC), committing to a peaceful resolution of their SCS disputes.[25] Among other commitments, the parties to the DoC agreed to 'reaffirm their respect for and commitment to the freedom of navigation in and overflight above the South China Sea as provided for by the universally recognised principles of international law, including the

---

[25] Declaration on the Conduct of Parties in the South China Sea, 4 November 2002, http://www.asean.org/asean/external-relations/china/item/declaration-on-the-conduct-of-parties-in-the-south-china-sea.

1982 UN Convention on the Law of the Sea' and to 'undertake to resolve their territorial and jurisdictional disputes by peaceful means, without resorting to the threat or use of force.'

As noted above, in 2011 and 2012 China repeatedly violated both the letter and spirit of the DoC by confronting, often with force or threat of force, Vietnamese and Philippine vessels operating lawfully in the SCS. China's rhetoric that it seeks only peaceful solutions to the SCS territorial and resource disputes is repeatedly belied by its aggression.

Perhaps realising that China has no intention of respecting its commitments under the DoC, the Philippines is currently attempting to employ another peaceful avenue—UNCLOS's mandatory dispute resolution mechanism—in an effort to resolve its SCS disputes with China. On 22 January 2013, the Philippines instituted an arbitral proceeding against China at the Permanent Court of Arbitration pursuant to UNCLOS, to which both China and the Philippines are parties.[26] Although disputes regarding sovereignty over the disputed land features in the SCS are not justiciable under UNCLOS proceedings, the Philippine arbitration case challenges the validity of China's nine-dash line and its assertion of sovereign rights and jurisdiction to essentially the entire SCS—a claim that is certainly justiciable under UNCLOS.

China, understanding the weakness of its nine-dash line assertion, predictably chose not to respect its commitments under UNCLOS to peaceful resolution of disputes through arbitration. Instead, Chinese officials flatly rejected the idea of arbitrating the case pursuant to UNCLOS, and accused the Philippines of violating 'the consensus enshrined' in the DoC.[27]

---

[26] The Republic of the Philippines v. The People's Republic of China, Permanent Court of Arbitration, http://www.pca-cpa.org/showpage.asp?pag_id=1529.

[27] "China rejects Philippines' arbitral request," *Xinhua*, 19 February 2013, http://www.chinadaily.com.cn/china/2013-02/19/content_16238133.htm.

A NATIONAL STRATEGY FOR THE SOUTH CHINA SEA

It behooves the US to lean forward in regard to its posture in the SCS. The US has national interests in the SCS and it cannot risk the possibility that ASEAN nations will agree to a code of conduct with China that is adverse to those interests. China's nine-dash line, which amounts to a twenty-first century *mare clausum* policy, must be aggressively countered. Given Chinese actions in recent years to advance its nine-dash line claim, nothing short of concrete US policy red lines will suffice.

In light of these circumstances, the US should develop and promulgate a National Strategy for the South China Sea (NSSCS) consisting of the following elements:

- Restatement of the US policy in the SCS: The NSSCS should first reiterate long-standing US policy priorities in the SCS. The US interests in the SCS include respect for international law, freedom of navigation, maintenance of security and stability, and unimpeded commerce and economic development.[28] While the US officials have made repeated statements communicating these interests, a written statement clarifying and expanding on these policies is overdue. For instance, the NSSCS must set forth in no uncertain terms the US position on the legality of military survey activities in China's EEZ and throughout the SCS.

- Stronger position regarding SCS land features: The US no longer has the luxury of staying out of SCS sovereignty disputes altogether. The acquisition of SCS land features has become a zero-sum game. For example, although Vietnam

---

[28] Odom, Jonathan G. "Where's the Stake? US Interests in the South China Sea," Third International Workshop of the East Sea (South China Sea) Studies (November 2011), http:// nghiencuubiendong.vn/en/conferences-and-seminars-/the-third-international-workshop-on-south-china-sea/671-wheres-the-stake-us-interests-in-the-south-china-sea-by-jonathan-g-odom.

and China dispute who has sovereignty over the Paracel Islands, China has effective control over the islands, and therefore, has enhanced its standing to enforce its excessive maritime claims in the waters surrounding the islands. Each coral reef or atoll in the SCS controlled by China is an additional land feature from which China may make excessive EEZ claims and disrupt the US military survey missions. As such, it is contrary to the US interests for China to gain control over additional SCS land features. Therefore, where sovereignty over particular land features is clear based on the available evidence, the US should make its opinion known. To continue to avoid such declarations is to risk further Chinese expansion of its excessive claims in the SCS.

- Increased freedom of navigation protests and naval operations: The US has repeatedly issued diplomatic protests (in 2001, 2002, and 2007) to China regarding its 'Order No. 75' which purports to restrict military surveys within its EEZ. The US Navy has also regularly conducted operational assertions (in fiscal years 2007-12) to protest China's policy.[29] These protests must, at a minimum, continue apace. But more frequent naval assertions are necessary. Optimally, such operations should be conducted with one or more of our allies in the region, such as Australia and Japan. Vietnam, whose commercial survey activities have been repeatedly interfered with by China, may also be willing to engage in joint operations with the US.

- Renewal of US State Department 'Limits in the Seas' reports: Until recently, the US regularly issued reports

---

[29] Maritime Claims Reference Manual, "China," http://www.jag.navy.mil/organization/code_10_mcrm.htm.

regarding various aspects of the law of the sea in regard to maritime claims made by foreign nations. Since 1970, the State Department published more than 125 reports regarding straight baseline claims, maritime and continental shelf borders, and territorial sea claims.[30] One section of the NSSCS should contain a legal review and rebuttal of China's excessive maritime claims in the SCS, including its nine-dash line map and domestic Chinese legislation that purports to restrict activities within its EEZ.

This section of the NSSCS should also be published separately as a 'Limits in the Seas' report and submitted to the UN *Law of the Sea Bulletin* for publication.[31] The State Department should consider producing separate reports regarding China's other excessive maritime claims concerning its contiguous zone and its attempt to draw baselines around the Senkaku Islands. The US should consider joining Japan's protest to the Commission on the Limits of the Continental Shelf regarding China's baseline claim of the Senkakus.[32]

- Preempt a SCS 'code of conduct' that violates the law of the sea: The firm legal positions taken by the US in its NSSCS will make it clear that it will not consent to a Code of Conduct for the SCS that violates either UNCLOS or customary international law. But the NSSCS should specifically note that any code of conduct that purports to restrict or prohibit military survey activities in the SCS or

---

[30] US Department of State, Bureau of Oceans and International Environmental and Scientific Affairs, Office of Ocean Affairs, *Limits in the Seas*, http://www.state.gov/e/oes/ocns/opa/c16065.htm. The last "Limits in the Seas" report was released in November 2005.

[31] UN website, "Law of the Sea Bulletins," http://www.un.org/depts/los/doalos_publications/los_bult.htm.

[32] Submission by the People's Republic of China to the Commission on the Limits of the Continental Shelf, 14 December 2012, http://www.un.org/depts/los/clcs_new/submissions_files/submission_chn_63_2012.htm.

within any EEZ is a non-starter for the US and that it will not comply with any such restriction.

- Assist SCS nations to comply with the law of the sea: The US must convince its friends and allies in the region to bring their domestic law and practice into compliance with the law of the sea. Several SCS nations (other than China) continue to make excessive maritime claims regarding access to their territorial sea and EEZ. Such claims permit China to take the position that it is acting in the same manner as its SCS neighbours. The US should, through bilateral negotiations, work with Malaysia, Vietnam, and the Philippines to abandon their excessive claims and thereby present a united front to legally isolate China.

- Support UNCLOS arbitration cases against China: The US should not remain a neutral observer to the ongoing arbitration case filed by the Philippines against China. It is in the US national interest that the arbitration be decided in the favour of the Philippines and against the nine-dash line claim made by China. Indeed, the US should urge other SCS nations—particularly Vietnam and Malaysia—to openly support the Philippines and to initiate arbitration cases of their own against China on the same legal grounds. Since Vietnam and Malaysia have chosen to be party to UNCLOS, they may as well take advantage of the opportunity to peacefully resolve the legality of China's claims in the SCS through arbitration. China will, undoubtedly, refuse to arbitrate with either nation, further isolating it from other SCS nations.

MANAGING BLOWBACK

China is likely to vigorously protest the release of a National Strategy for the SCS. After all, Chinese officials complain when the US officials merely restate long-standing and uncontroversial policies in the region. For example, in July 2011, Secretary of State Hillary Clinton stated that the US opposes 'the threat or use of force by any claimant in the South China Sea to advance its claims or interfere with legitimate economic activity.'[33] Despite the fact that Clinton's statement fell well within the four corners of the Declaration of Conduct, Chinese Foreign Minister Yang Jiechi called her comments an 'attack' on China.[34] Any Chinese protests over a National Strategy document should be treated as disingenuous posturing.

First of all, the US has in the past promulgated comprehensive policy statements regarding the Asia-Pacific region.[35] During the 1990s, the Department of Defense (DoD) issued four 'East Asia Strategy Reports' to 'explain DoD's security strategy for the region to Congress, our allies and friends, and the American public.'[36] The 1990 and 1992 reports outlined the US military's proposed changes in global strategy and force structure in response to the end of the Cold War, while the 1995 and 1998 reports reaffirmed the US security commitments to the region and stated an intention to maintain approximately 100,000 military personnel there.[37] In regard to the SCS, the 1995 report stated, 'The UN has urged peaceful settlement of SCS issues, and strongly opposes the threat or use of military force to assert any nation's claim.'[38]

---

[33] Clinton, Hillary Rodham. Press Statement, 22 July 2011, http://www.state.gov/secretary/rm/2011/07/168989.htm.

[34] "China: US comments on South China Sea are an 'attack'", *Associated Press*, 25 July 2010, http://www.thejakartapost.com/news/2010/07/25/china-us-comments-s-china-sea-are-039attack039.html.

[35] Cronin, Patrick M. "Contested Waters: Managing Disputes in the East and South China Seas," *Bulletin 6*, Center for a New American Security (December 2012), http://www.cnas.org/files/documents/publications/CNAS_Bulletin_Cronin_ContestedWaters.pdf.

[36] US Department of Defense, News Release, 27 February 1995, http://www.defense.gov/releases/release.aspx?releaseid=380.

[37] US Department of Defense, "The United States Security Strategy for the East Asia-Pacific Region" (1998), p. 5.

[38] *Ibid.*, p. 20.

More recently in January 2012, the Defense Department released two strategy and budget documents, making clear the US' intentions to place greater emphasis on the Asia-Pacific region.[39] As such, whether in the Asia-Pacific or another strategic region, it is hardly unprecedented that the US should promulgate a comprehensive policy statement regarding its strategic interests in the SCS.

Moreover, China cannot be heard to complain about the US declaring and pursuing its interests in the SCS, given China's clear intentions towards the Arctic—a region that is far from its shores. China has vigorously pursued its purported interests in the Arctic. In a March 2010 speech to the Peoples' Political Consultative Conference, a retired rear admiral of the Chinese People's Liberation Army (PLA) Navy, Yin Zhuo, declared that 'The Arctic belongs to all the people around the world as no nation has sovereignty over it.'[40]

Chinese Arctic specialists have described China as a 'near-Arctic state' and a 'stakeholder' in Arctic affairs.[41] Other Arctic nations, including the US, apparently agree with China, and granted it 'ad hoc' observer at the Arctic Council in 2007 and permanent observer status in May 2013.

US RATIFICATION OF UNCLOS UNNECESSARY

No argument regarding the US policy concerning the SCS may be made without begging the question whether the US should accede to UNCLOS. Proponents of the US accession claim that the US cannot

[39] US Department of Defense, *Sustaining US Global Leadership: Priorities for 21st Century Defense* (January 2012), and *Defense Budget: Priorities and Choices* (January 2012). For a comprehensive review of the US posture towards China, see O'Rourke, Ronald, "China Naval Modernization: Implications for US Navy Capabilities – Background and Issues for Congress," Congressional Research Service, 5 September 2013, http://www.fas.org/sgp/crs/row/RL33153.pdf.

[40] Saran, Shyam. "India's stake in Arctic cold war," *The Hindu*, 2 February 2012, http://www.thehindu.com/opinion/op-ed/article2848280.ece.

[41] Guilford, Gwynn. "What Is China's Arctic Game Plan?," *The Atlantic*, 16 May 2013, http://www.theatlantic.com/china/archive/2013/05/what-is-chinas-arctic-game-plan/275894/.

advance and protect its interests in the SCS unless it accedes to the convention. Indeed, UNCLOS is often promoted by its proponents as a panacea, and that the US membership would be determinative in any number of maritime controversies, including Chinese aggression in the SCS.

But the navigational rights and freedoms enjoyed by the US are advanced not by membership in a treaty, but rather by maintaining a strong navy, defending long-standing legal principles, and conducting persistent naval operations. Specifically, the US relies on the customary international law of the sea (which happens to be codified in UNCLOS) and the US Freedom of Navigation Program to protect its rights and freedoms. Securing the US interests in the SCS depends on these factors, not on membership in UNCLOS.

The customary international law of the sea existed long before UNCLOS and includes the principles of freedom of navigation and overflight on the high seas, 'innocent passage' through territorial waters, and passage rights through international straits and archipelagos. The convention merely codified and elaborated upon these widely accepted principles. Under the Freedom of Navigation Program, the US challenges excessive maritime claims made by China and other coastal states in contravention of customary international law, as that law is reflected in UNCLOS. The US' efforts combine diplomatic protests and military operations to preserve the US navigational rights.

The US Navy thrived for more than 180 years from its birth in 1775 through two world wars, developing into a global maritime power, all without the benefit of a written convention on the law of the sea. In 1958, the principles of high seas freedom and innocent passage through territorial waters were codified in the first round of law of the sea conventions. Between 1958 and 1982, the Navy continued to fulfill its mission on a global scale. UNCLOS was adopted in 1982, duplicating the navigational provisions of the 1958 conventions and 'crystallizing' the concepts of transit passage and archipelagic sea-lane passage. Since 1982, through the end of the Cold War and to the present day, the Navy continues to prosecute its mission as the world's preeminent naval power.

The US, in contrast to China and several other SCS nations, complies with the navigational norms, maritime boundary limits, and all other customary international law as reflected in UNCLOS. China and other SCS nations are the scofflaws, not the US. By forgoing UNCLOS membership, the US is in no way hindering its ability to secure, preserve, or otherwise protect its navigational rights and freedoms in the SCS.

CONCLUSION

Chinese intentions in the SCS are clear—a steady acquisition of land features for the purpose of establishing a massive EEZ throughout the SCS, thereby justifying its nine-dash line claim. As it continues to expand its civilian police and military fleets, China will be in a strong position to harass and interfere with the US military survey activities in the SCS.

China's nine-dash line must be met with a US red line, and sooner rather than later. The US should act firmly and decisively while it can exercise military superiority in the Asia-Pacific region in general and the SCS in particular. A National Strategy for the SCS is an important first step in changing the current momentum in the SCS from one in which China persistently bullies its smaller neighbours into surrendering land features into one in which China must adapt its behaviour to comply with international law.

Steven Groves is the Bernard and Barbara Lomas Senior Research Fellow in the Margaret Thatcher Center for Freedom at The Heritage Foundation in Washington, DC, and is leader of Heritage's Freedom Project.

APPENDIX A

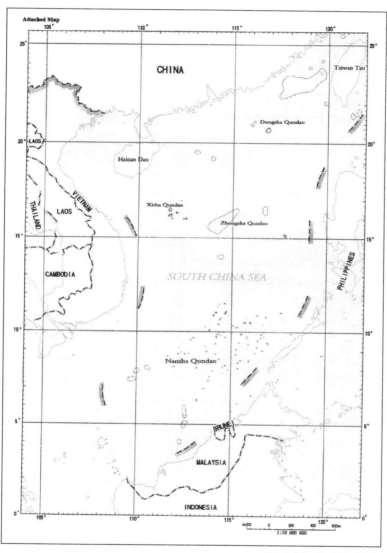

China's "Nine-Dash Line" Claim
Made by China on May 7, 2009

APPENDIX B

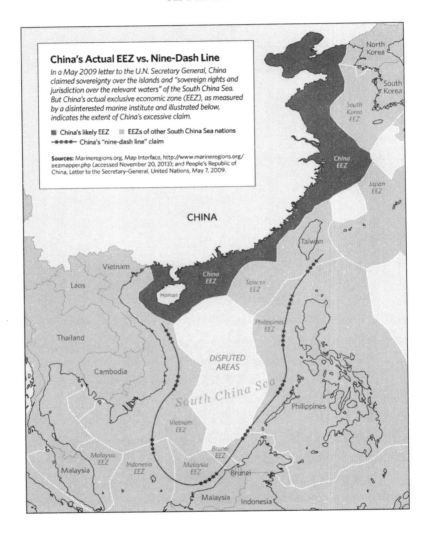

China's Actual EEZ vs. Nine-Dash Line

In a May 2009 letter to the U.N. Secretary General, China claimed sovereignty over the islands and "sovereign rights and jurisdiction over the relevant waters" of the South China Sea. But China's actual exclusive economic zone (EEZ), as measured by a disinterested marine institute and illustrated below, indicates the extent of China's excessive claim.

■ China's likely EEZ   ■ EEZs of other South China Sea nations
━━━ China's "nine-dash line" claim

Sources: Marineregions.org, Map Interface, http://www.marineregions.org/eezmapper.php (accessed November 20, 2013); and People's Republic of China, Letter to the Secretary-General, United Nations, May 7, 2009.

CHAPTER 7

India–China Land Border Disputes

RN Ravi

India and China, the two most populous countries, with world's largest militaries, are locked in volatile land border disputes for more than half a century. The border tensions between the two had escalated into a full-scale war in 1962. Since then sporadic armed face-offs between the troops of the two countries are not infrequent. Notwithstanding several mutually arrived agreements and protocols in the last two decades, some 4,000 km 'India–China' border remains highly sensitive and prone to armed confrontations. Some of these have the potential to escalate into major conflagrations with far reaching geopolitical, geo-economic and military consequences for the region and beyond.

Until military occupation of Tibet by China in 1950, India's border with China was limited to the one between Ladakh and the tenuously held Chinese province Sinkiang, now Xinjiang, in the stretch between the tri-junctions of India-Afghanistan-China and India-Tibet-China.

India had a traditionally settled and age-old friendly border with Tibet. Trades between India and Tibet flourished. Traders, pilgrims, scholars, artisans, and explorers moved across the border with ease. While the Tibetans, since millennia, thronged every year for pilgrimage at Bodh Gaya and Sarnath in India, the holiest of places for the Buddhists across the world, Indian pilgrims visited Mount Kailash-Kang Rimpoche and Mansarovar Lake, the mythical abode of Lord Siva, the most revered deity of the Hindu pantheon.

Nalanda University in India was a vibrant centre of scholarship in the first millennia where liberal arts, science and philosophies, attracted a large number of Tibetan scholars and students. Guru Padmasambhava, Dharmakirti, Rinchen Tsangpo, Atisha and Milarepa among the pioneer scholars and Buddhist saints of India carried the teachings of Buddha and Buddhist practices to Tibet.

When the invading Turks from Central Asia in the twelfth century destroyed the Nalanda University and unleashed unspeakable mayhem and killings, its remaining scholars and artifacts moved to sanctuaries in Tibet.

During the long subjugation of India by Muslim invaders from Central Asia, some of its cultural and intellectual heritage were relocated in Tibet for safety and continuity. Indian students and scholars went to Tibet in pursuit of their intellectual and spiritual quests.

When Communist China invaded and occupied Tibet, Tibetan spiritual leaders, scholars and lay people escaped to safety in India to preserve their culture, traditions and spiritual heritage from cultural genocide and religious persecutions. While China, during the Cultural Revolution, wreaked massive destruction on iconic cultural and religious institutions and symbols in Tibet, the expatriate Tibetans replicated them in India to thwart extinction of their unique identity. The fourteenth Dalai Lama, the spiritual and temporal head of Tibet, other high lineage holder Lamas of different strands of Tibetan Buddhism and some 1,50,000 Tibetans found a welcoming home in India.

The two countries shared a profound cultural, intellectual and emotional cosmology. The long political border between them was friendly and seldom a source of tension.

India's border with Sinkiang, tenuously held by imperial China, ran along the crest of the high mountain ranges, Kuen Lun, Karakoram, Mustagh to Tangdumbash Plains between the Sarikol and Mustagh Atta Ranges north of the Kilik-Mintaka Pass up to India-Afghanistan-China tri-junction. It was to the west of India-Tibet-China tri-junction near the point eighty degree east. The region of Sinkiang was ruled by a number of warlords who for the greater part of recorded history kept fighting with each other and could not be subjugated by China.

The region of Sinkiang was so volatile that in 1860 when the travellers and traders from Shahidullah, Malikshai and adjoining areas oppressed by the marauding gangs appealed to the central Sinkiang authorities for taking these areas under them, the latter declined on the ground that these areas fell beyond the jurisdiction of Sinkiang. Since the virulent lawlessness seriously affected trades between India and Yarkand in Sinkiang region, India subdued the marauders, extended its administration up to Shahidullah and enforced peace along the trade routes.

In the eighteenth century, Imperial Russia had expanded its empire into Central Asia up to the north-western border of Sinkiang. The emerging geopolitical and strategic environment in the region on account of Russian expansion kept the Indian and Chinese authorities worried. China was not in a position to offer any credible resistance to Russia's potential march through Sinkiang to the borders of India. The British Indian authorities responded by ceding the area north of watershed of Kuen Lun Range under India's control to Sinkiang and sought to turn imperial China into its ally. In the strategic calculus of the British, imperial China, smarting under humiliating defeat in the

Opium War and subsequent wars with Britain and resultant unequal treaties, could be comforted with this territorial gift and be a buffer between India and Russia.

It is an irony of history that when China's hold over its western most province was tenuous and often teetered on collapse by internal rebellions, it was India that lent the most needed strategic and tactical help to China in consolidating its position there. But Communist China betrayed a nascent independent India committed to world peace by militarily grabbing some forty thousand sq km of India's land in Aksai Chin in 1962 and further annexing some five thousand one hundred sq km of its land west of the Karakoram Pass through an illegal treaty with Pakistan in March 1963.

Pakistan, soon after its creation, had surreptitiously moved its armed militia (Rangers) into Kashmir and Ladakh in 1948 and grabbed a large chunk of India's land. While the issue was yet not resolved between India and Pakistan, China fished in the troubled waters and took away a part of it through an illegal treaty with Pakistan and built strategic infrastructures including roads linking Xinjiang to Tibet and rest of China besides access to the Arabian Sea and strategic assets around it. China as quid pro quo rewarded Pakistan with military nuclear proliferation.

The history of the north-western frontier of India with Tibet and China in the first millennia have been elaborately recorded in Ladakhi chronicles. Reputed historians including AH Francke, Luciano Petech and Z Ahmad translated these historical documents that vividly described the geopolitical developments and power struggles between India, Tibet and China during the T'ang dynasty (AD 618-907). China's efforts to keep control over its far-south-western areas of Turkestan (Sinkiang) involved sporadic clashes and cooperation with rulers of west Tibet and Ladakh of India. Baltistan, Gilgit and Ladakh regions of India served as buffer between China and Tibet.

Margaret W Fisher, Leo E Rose and Robert A Huttenback, famous historians have recorded in their book *Himalayan Battleground*, 'even the most exuberant Chinese historians have never claimed that Tibet was part of China in the tenth century'.

The fact of a settled border between India and Tibet since ancient times is amply borne out by the vastly recorded and oral histories of the two countries and their people. In the pre-modern era, in absence of advanced scientific cartographic tools and techniques, the borders were mutually defined with help of natural markers—passes in the mountain ranges and the courses of rivers. Traders traversing the border paid levies to the foreign governments. Adventurers and pilgrims from either side entered the other's territory after obtaining required permits, visas, from the respective governments. There were traditionally established trade marts on Indian and Tibetan sides of the border. In the high altitude mountainous terrain, yaks and horses were the carriers of goods. There was a flourishing class of auxiliary traders: Local nomads on both sides who rented their yaks and horses for the trade. Since the trade and pilgrimage involved long distance travels along the traditional foot-trails, several villages en-route were used for rest and recuperation. All these activities sustained and enhanced local economies of the people of the two countries.

Instances of localised clashes between the adjacent local rulers of the two countries were few and far between. In one such recorded clash, Tibetan forces captured parts of eastern Ladakh in 1639. However, in 1684 the Tibetans were pushed back to Tashigong, the traditional India–Tibet border in this sector. The Treaty of Tingmosgang was signed in 1684 delineating the border between India and Tibet in this sector at Lha-ri stream, a tributary of the Indus river five miles south west of Demchok. Under this treaty, India got the trading monopoly of export of shawl wool from west Tibet and the Dalai Lama obtained monopoly of trading in brick tea with India. For the subsequent nearly three centuries the treaty was respected, the integrity of the border was observed in letter and spirit both by India and Tibet until Communist China attacked India in 1962 and captured Demchok after it had invaded and captured Tibet in 1950. The Chinese invasions negatively altered the geopolitical ecology of the entire India–Tibet border region and the centuries of peace was shattered.

Detailed accounts by European travellers, adventurers and historians of the region bear ample evidence to the fact that India and Tibet had a peaceful border and commerce between the two flourished. Caravans of traders carrying goods from both sides frequently visited the trading marts of each other and paid levies to the respective governments.

William Moorcroft, superintendent of the East India Company's stud, visited Ladakh on way to Yarkand in 1820-22 on a dual commission: One by the Company to purchase Turkman horses for its cavalry and another by the British merchants of Calcutta to establish a commercial intercourse with north-western parts of Asia, extensively recorded the nature and extent of Ladakh's border with Tibet and China. He found a vibrant trade between the three countries—India's Ladakh, Tibet and Yarkand in Turkmenistan over which China exercised only a tenuous control. Leh in Ladakh was a large trading hub. Moorcroft in his letters to the Company clearly mentioned the Aksai Chin area as being under India. He also mentioned how the trade routes through the Aksai Chin traversing between India and Turkistan, now called Xinjiang by China, and to Tibet were administered by India.

The population on both sides of the India–Tibet border was largely nomadic. Their main economic activity was tending the livestock—sheep, goats and yaks. The pastures of India and Tibet, some of them straddling the border between the two countries, were well recognised by nomads of both the countries. These pastures were administered according to the customary laws and practices. The nomads residing in border areas, in seasons, used to take, without let or hindrance, their livestock to pastures in the other country. Direction of such seasonal movements of livestock was locational. The country whose pastures were customarily used by the nomads of the other country annually received a pre-determined amount in kind or cash by the government of the other country. This annual payment was called 'posa'.

The region of India extending to the India-Tibet-China tri-junction is a vast expanse of over 40,000 square kms of high lands that includes Aksai Chin, Soda Plains and Lingzi-thang. The extreme climate renders the region incapable of sustaining more than a meagre population. Important trade routes linking India, Tibet and Sinkiang traversed through this cold mountain dessert. These routes, besides being the lifelines of regional trades between the three countries—India, Tibet and China (Sinkiang)—were the feeders to the traditional Silk Route, which was a set of arterial and capillary routes linking countries and civilisations from the Mediterranean Sea to the East, South and Southeast Asia.

Refinements in cartographic technologies since the seventeenth century made it possible to have more defined maps of the borders. Maps drawn by India, Tibet and China in the nineteenth and early twentieth centuries bear evidence to the defined borders of India with these countries. Over 150 years after the Treaty of Tingmosgang in 1684, the Treaty of September 1842 over trade between Ladakh region of India and Tibet reaffirmed the traditionally settled border between the two countries in the western sector of India–Tibet border. WH Johnson, a British official of the Trigonometrical Survey of India was entrusted a commission in July 1865 to explore the country of Khotan farther north of Kuen Lun ranges, a territory then under the local ruler of Kashmir and Ladakh and currently in Xinjiang. Johnson affirmed that the area of Aksai Chin was part of India and that the customary boundary of India was well-known and respected by the neighbouring rulers, traders and travellers.

The Gazetteer of Kashmir & Ladakh, 1891, delineated in details the borders of Ladakh region of India with Tibet and the Sinkiang province of China. The map clearly showed the Aksai Chin, Lingzi-thang and Changchenmo areas as parts of India.

The China government shared its map with the Indian Consul at Kashgar (Sinkiang) in 1893 through its representative Hung Ta-chen delineating the borders between India and China. This map accepts the Aksai Chin as part of India and it conformed to India's traditional border alignment with China as shown in the map attached with the Gazetteer of Kashmir & Ladakh. The postal map of China published by the Government of China in Peking in 1917 further re-affirmed the Aksai Chin as part of India.

The eastern sector of India–Tibet border lies between tri-junctions of India-Bhutan-Tibet in the west and India-Myanmar-Tibet in the east. China was nowhere in proximity of this border though occasionally they made light forays into Tibet from their Sichuan bases but had no interaction or exchanges with India.

This segment of the border was quieter than the western segment. In contrast to the western segment that had facilitated vibrant commercial and sociological interactions between India, Tibet and China and served as trade corridors to the Central Asia, the eastern segment was largely non-eventful. It was so primarily due to the distinct socioeconomic and cultural cosmology of the Indian tribes inhabiting the region south of India–Tibet border from the Tibetans. These indigenous Indian tribes did not have much interaction with Tibet.

Along the over 1,100 kms of India–Tibet border in this segment, there is a pocket near the tri-junction of India-Bhutan-Tibet where the people of the three countries shared common socio-ethnic, religious and linguistic coordinates.

The people inhabiting the India-Bhutan-Tibet tri-junction followed the Vajrayana tradition of Buddhism. This tradition was the product of spiritual, philosophical and intellectual churning at the Nalanda University in the first millennia. From there it was carried to Tibet where it became the predominant tradition. One of the routes followed by the scholars from Nalanda to reach Tibet was through Bhutan. The people along the route embraced the Vajrayana tradition and several monasteries of this tradition sprung up in the region over time.

When the Turks from Central Asia invaded India and attacked the famous Nalanda University in the twelfth century, several scholars and artifacts of Buddhism shifted from India to Tibet. The centre of gravity of the Vajrayana tradition moved from India to Tibet. The state patronage of Buddhism in Tibet helped robust growth of monasteries and related institutions of Vajrayana tradition there. The people living at the India-Bhutan-Tibet tri-junction were greatly inspired and influenced by these institutions. A monastery was built on Indian side (Tawang) of the tri-junction in the seventeenth century. With the patronage of the 5th Dalai Lama's Drepung monastery in Tibet, it grew into the largest monastery in the area. Vibrant theological and intellectual exchanges took place between the Tawang monastery in India and the Drepung monastery in Tibet. The affinity between the two monasteries was so intense that when the 5th Dalai Lama passed away, Tsangyang, a boy born near Tawang was anointed the 6th Dalai Lama. Notwithstanding intense ethno-religious kinship between the people of India, Tibet and Bhutan, their political boundaries were well understood.

Indigenous Indian tribes, untouched by centuries of vigorous cultural and religious exchanges between India and Tibet through Bhutan, inhabited east of the India-Bhutan-Tibet tri-junction.

These tribes were more inward looking. Their faiths were indigenous. Their socioeconomic interactions were largely southward with the people inhabiting the plains and foothills of Assam.

India's historically consistent approach towards them has been one of soft engagement. Their patterns of life and livelihoods were not disrupted and their customs and traditions were respected by the state. The British, too, when they took over this part of India in the mid nineteenth century, did not tinker with the age-old tradition of the state, maintaining a dis-engaged grip over them. After the British left India in 1947, the post-colonial India institutionalised this tradition of substantive autonomy to the ethnic tribes by providing safeguards in its Constitution.

Unlike the western sector of the India–Tibet border, the eastern segment did not have any worthwhile commercial exchanges. Except for a few adventurers, trans-border movements were very limited and that too only among those living in close proximity of the border. It was, by and large, a passive border with no history of conflict or border dispute until China moved in Tibet.

Strategic manoeuvres of imperial Russia in Central Asia that had reached almost at the western segment of the India–Tibet border and rise of a rabidly nationalist China on the east after the fall of Manchus in the early twentieth century kept India and Tibet worried. The fast unfolding geopolitical and strategic scenario was freighted with sinister forebodings both for India and Tibet. The imperial Russia and the ultra-nationalist republican China had to be preempted in their potential misadventures toward India and Tibet. Convergence of the strategic interests of India and Tibet led to the Simla Convention between Great Britain, Tibet and China in 1914. The British persuaded the Chinese to come to the table. The Convention reaffirmed the traditional alignment of the India–Tibet border in the eastern sector. The so-called McMahon Line, that formally delineated the India–Tibet border in the east, was a mere reiteration of the long settled traditional border alignment.

The Simla Convention also delineated Tibet's border with China. The sprawling Tibet was segmented into Inner and Outer Tibets. Inner Tibet was its eastern most part in close proximity to China where the Chinese historically exercised some kind of authority and thus, it was made a part of the People's Republic of China with a proviso that Tibet would continue exercising its traditional right to appoint the 'high priests' to the monasteries in Inner Tibet and also having 'full rights' in matters affecting religious institutions therein. At the same time, independence of the Outer Tibet was recognised. China gave an explicit commitment not to invade or intrude it and not to 'convert Tibet into a Chinese province'.

China actively participated in the deliberations and agreed to the outcomes of the Convention. Their representative, Ivan Chen, had initialed the Convention documents including the maps. However, on later instructions from Beijing, he did not sign it. Apparently, China had misgivings about the line delineating Inner and Outer Tibet. However, China's refusal to sign the documents did not undermine the fact that there was no difference over the alignment of the India–Tibet border.

Although the age-old friendly relations between India and Tibet precluded any need for regular border policing by either country, India could not be oblivious to the fast emerging profound geopolitical and strategic developments in its northern neighbourhood. India took measures to establish its visible administrative presence at least at some strategically important points along the traditional India–Tibet border that was hitherto lightly administered. India began sending periodic patrols to the routes and tracks traversing between the two countries. Indian patrols had friendly exchanges with the Tibetan border authorities. Given the friendly relations between the countries, these were police patrols and not the army.

The invasion and occupation of Tibet by Communist China in 1950 shattered the millennia old peace and tranquility at the India–Tibet border. The newly established Communist regime in Beijing seemed determined to restore the real or imagined frontiers of the imperial China. It fought a war with the US in Korea and confronted it over Taiwan. It unilaterally reinterpreted imperial China's Cho-yon relationship with Tibet that was broadly in the nature of China extending military support to Tibet in case of external aggression on it in return for the independent Tibet extending its spiritual mentorship to the Imperial Court. Such a relationship between the two developed in the seventeenth century and continued thereafter. Imperial China respected the independence of Tibet and never sought to integrate it in its empire. Tibet, in exercise of its sovereignty, entered into treaties with other countries. However, Communist China in its drive to restore, indeed expand its frontiers, interpreted this relationship in furtherance of its imperial ambitions.

While the world's attention was focused on the conflict in Korean peninsula where the US troops under the command of General Douglas MacArthur had crossed the 38th parallel on 7 October 1950, the same day over 40,000 Chinese troops from the South-West Military Region under command of Gen Zhang Guohua crossed the Drichu river and marched into Tibet. The People's Liberation Army (PLA) captured Lhasa and spread itself over the strategic vintages in Tibet. Tibet lost its independence and India got a new neighbour in China.

The sudden turn of events severely impacted the geopolitical and strategic imperatives of India's northern frontier. China, by force, converted the age-old India–Tibet border into 'India–China' border. Anticipating resistance from the freedom loving Tibetans, it heavily militarised the hitherto peaceful India–Tibet border. At that time, India's defence infrastructure at the border was almost non-existent.

Age-old mutual friendship between India and Tibet precluded any need for military deployment along the border. The mutual trust was such that the two countries did not even keep their regular police posts along the border. Except a thin presence of regulatory authorities at the trade routes, any other deployment of border guarding resources was considered wasteful and scrupulously avoided.

Although independent India and Communist China came into being almost about the same time, the fundamentally distinct processes of their coming into being shaped their world views differently. While India's freedom struggle under Mahatma Gandhi, the biggest apostle of peace in modern world history, was non-violent and peaceful, Communist China was born through a protracted bloody revolution under the leadership of Mao. While the leaders of India's Freedom Struggle carried the message of peace and peaceful coexistence to all the people in the world, Mao believed in exporting bloody revolutions, especially in its neighbourhood countries, in order to destabilise them and turn them into its lackey regimes.

Forcible occupation of Tibet and brutal suppression of religious practices by Communist China rankled the Tibetan nationalists. The Dalai Lama accompanied by several thousand Tibetans escaped to India. India, in keeping with its tradition of warm hospitality to guests and consistent with age-old friendship with Tibet, received the Dalai Lama and his entourage with warmth and extended all possible humanitarian assistance to them. China blamed India for giving refuge to the Dalai Lama and several thousand Tibetans who fled to India. It assumed a menacingly aggressive posture along India's border.

China began their hostile military manoeuvres along India's border and grabbed Indian territories—mountain features, valleys and passes with a view to denying India the strategic territorial depths imperative for its defence against future Chinese assaults. It built massive strategic infrastructures along India–Tibet border. It sought to destabilise India's northern frontiers to undermine its potential to assist the Tibetan nationalists in the event of a likely uprising in Tibet.

The PLA had invaded Tibet from the east. Subduing the vast and arid Tibetan plateau in the west, Tibet was a daunting military challenge to them. They needed an assured military reinforcement to quell rebellions in west Tibet. Reinforcement from the remote east could be slow and vulnerable to Tibetan resistance. A reliable route for military reinforcement and logistic supply from Xinjiang was a tempting option for China. Between Tibet and Xinjiang lies the strategic Indian territory of Aksai Chin. Taking advantage of the very thin Indian presence in the area, China surreptitiously grabbed Aksai Chin in early 1950s and converted the trade route between Tibet and Xinjiang passing through it into a military logistic supply line.

When India raised the issue of land grab, China responded saying that the border was 'not defined'. India produced ample evidence to convince China that the border was traditionally well settled. However, China ignored the historical evidences. Under the cover of 'undefined' border, the PLA continued grabbing the Indian territory. They obstructed the Indian border patrols in their routine movements. On 21 October 1959, the Chinese Army ambushed and killed an Indian police patrol party near Konka Pass opening into the Aksai Chin.

The Chinese premier Chou En-Lai, during his New Delhi visit in April 1960, in utter disregard to historical facts, claimed that China's border with India in the north-western sector was not along the Kuen Lun mountain range to the east of Karakoram Pass but it followed the crest of the Karakoram mountain range that shortly after the Karakoram Pass swerved south-east into the Soda Plains.

The Konka Pass is near the tail end of the Karakoram pass. This claim would take away almost over 40,000 sq kms, entire Aksai Chin, of India.

On 20 October 1962, China launched an all out attack all along the border on an unsuspecting India. Taking advantage of its superior military assets and elements of surprise, it grabbed large tracts of India's land in all the sectors of the border. Although the war was supposed to have ended with a formal ceasefire on 21 November 1962, China not only kept occupation of large tracts of Indian territory grabbed in the war but also continued with menacing belligerent postures all along the Line of Actual Control (LAC).

Beside direct military action along the border, China launched a proxy war on India by strategically arming Pakistan including illicit transfer of military nuclear technology to it and instigating tribal secessionist insurgencies in India's Northeast.

It sheltered the Indian rebels, armed them and trained them in guerrilla warfare. The military headquarters of the tribal rebels of Northeast India—the National Socialist Council of Nagaland, the United Liberation Front of Asom, the Peoples' Liberation Army of Manipur and National Democratic Front of Bodoland, are located in Yunan province of China and their liaison offices are in Kunming city. China works for their strategic and tactical synergy from time to time, replenishes and upgrades their military ordnance, and runs safe houses for this purpose at the towns along its border with Myanmar.

China is yet to respond with sincerity to India's peaceful initiatives to settle the border dispute. Ironically, ever since early 1990s when India engaged China for settling the border dispute through dialogue, China has escalated its belligerence at the border. It has refused to agree on a LAC that could be the basis for freezing its further military adventures. It keeps a dynamic notion of its LAC as it helps it in grabbing more and more Indian territory. Despite sixteen rounds of talks at the level of special representatives in the last one decade, Chinese military adventurism towards India remains unabated.

China seems determined to undermine through military means India's potential rise as a democratically sensitive, economically prosperous and responsible world power. China's growing belligerence towards India is consistent with their manifest imperialistic ambition to be the military hegemon in the Indo-Pacific region.

RN Ravi is former Special Director of the Intelligence Bureau of India.

BIBLIOGRAPHY

1. *Himalayan Frontiers* by Dorothy Woodman
2. *History of the Frontier Areas Bordering Assam* by Sir Robert Reid
3. *The North-East Frontier of India* by Alexander Mackenzie
4. *Protracted Contest, Sino-Indian Rivalry in the Twentieth Century* by John W Garver
5. *The Status of Tibet, History, Rights, and Prospects in International Law* by Michael C van Walt van Praag
6. *The Dragon In The Land of Snows, A history of Modern Tibet Since 1947* by Tsering Shakya
7. *A History of Modern Tibet, 1913-1951* by Melvyn C Goldstein
8. *My Years With Nehru, The Chinese Betrayal* by BN Mullik
9. *On China* by Henry Kissinger
10. *The White House Years* by Henry Kissinger
11. Chou en-Lai's Press Conference, Hsinhua News Agency, 30 April 1960
12. Moorcroft Papers, I.O.L. Eur. MSS. Folio 31. G.28.p.141
13. *The Founding of the Kashmir State* by KM Panikkar
14. *The China–India Border, the Origins of the Disputed Boundaries* by Alastair Lamb
15. Gazetteer of Kashmir& Ladakh, 1891
16. White Paper II Nehru to Chou En lai 26 September 1959
17. White Paper III Chou En Lai to Nehru 7 November 1959
18. *Himalayan Battle ground* by Fisher, Rose and Huttenback
19. Johnson WH, R.G.s.J Volume 37, 1867

CHAPTER 8

Sino-Indian Border Tensions and the US–Asia Rebalance

Lisa Curtis

India is keeping a wary eye on China's rapid global ascent. Unresolved border issues that led to a Sino-Indian War in 1962 have been heating up again in recent years. In April 2013, the most serious border incident between India and China in over two decades occurred when Chinese troops settled for three weeks several miles inside Indian territory on the Depsang Plains in Ladakh. India must increasingly factor the potential threat of conflict over its disputed borders with China into its security planning and projections.

While Indian strategists assess that Pakistan poses the most immediate threat to India, they increasingly view China as the more important long-term strategic threat. Last year, former Indian ambassador to the US, Nirupama Rao, acknowledged that China's military modernisation had brought a new security calculus to the region. While Indian officials were initially cautious in their response to the US policy of rebalancing toward the Asia-Pacific, continued

Chinese provocations along their disputed border would likely prompt New Delhi to become more open to the idea of a robust US role in the region.

HARDENING CHINESE POSITION

Long-standing border disputes between China and India continue to cause friction between the two countries despite ongoing border talks that started in the 1980s. India claims that China occupies more than 14,000 square miles of Indian territory in the Aksai Chin along its northern border in Kashmir (commonly referred to as the western sector), while China lays claim to more than 34,000 square miles of India's Northeastern state of Arunachal Pradesh (commonly referred to as the eastern sector). The Chinese Communist Party has never accepted the validity of the McMahon Line as the demarcation of the Sino-Indian border in Tibet.

The two sides fought a brief border war in 1962 after China invaded the eastern and western sectors of their shared borders and ended up annexing the area of Aksai Chin, a barren plateau that had been part of the pre-Partition princely state of Jammu and Kashmir. India, also, is a long-term host to the Dalai Lama, the Tibetan spiritual leader, and more than 150,000 Tibetan refugees many of whom fled after China annexed Tibet in 1950. In 1993, the two sides signed a 'Peace and Tranquility' agreement which suggested no use of force, and in 1996, they concluded a military agreement in which they spelled out confidence building measures including interaction between border personnel.

Despite the progress in border negotiations in the 1990s, talks between their respective 'special representatives' (former Indian National Security Advisor Shivshankar Menon and Chinese State Councillor Yang Jiechi) have achieved little in the last decade. Aside from clarifying the mapping of the middle sector of their disputed frontiers (the border that demarcates the Indian state of Sikkim), the talks have remained deadlocked over the status of the eastern and western sectors.

China has taken a tougher position on their border disputes in recent years. Beijing regularly takes steps that call into question Indian sovereignty over the states of Arunachal Pradesh and Jammu and Kashmir, and has stepped up probing operations along different parts of their shared frontier. The Chinese are also building up military infrastructure and expanding a network of road, rail, and air links in the border areas. Beijing has fortified its military capabilities in Tibet and now has at least five fully-operational airbases there, an extensive rail network and over 36,000 miles of roads. This allows China the ability to move several divisions of troops as well as weapons and armoured vehicles to the Line of Actual Control (LAC) in a relatively short period of time.

The hardening Chinese position can be traced back to comments made by the Chinese ambassador to India, referring to the entire state of Arunachal Pradesh as part of China, in the run-up to former Chinese President Hu Jintao's November 2006 visit to India.[1] The Chinese ambassador's statement was followed by an increasing number of Chinese media reports referring to Arunachal Pradesh as 'Southern Tibet'. Prior to 2005, there were no Chinese references to 'Southern Tibet' in China's official media.[2] In 2009, China opposed an Asian Development Bank (ADB) loan, part of which was earmarked for a watershed project in Arunachal Pradesh—another demonstration that China is questioning Indian sovereignty over the state more openly.

---

[1] Curtis, Lisa. "US–India Relations: The China Factor," *Heritage Foundation Backgrounder No. 2209,* 25 November 2008, http://www.heritage.org/Research/Reports/2008/11/US-India-Relations-The-China-Factor.

[2] Malik, Mohan. "China Unveils 'The Kashmir Card,'" *China Brief, Vol. 10, No. 19* (24 September 2010), http://www.jamestown.org/programs/chinabrief/single/?tx_ttnews%5Btt_news%5D=36915&tx_ttnews%5BbackPid%5D=25&cHash=078d3aabd3.

India, says China, has backtracked on their 2005 'Agreement on Political Parameters and Guiding Principles for Settlement of the Boundary Question'. The 2005 accord stipulated that 'settled populations will not be disturbed.'[3] India argues that China has violated this part of the agreement by laying claim to Tawang in Arunachal Pradesh. Chinese interlocutors claim Tawang is part of Tibet because one of the Dalai Lamas was born there.[4] The Chinese have objected to visits to Tawang by the Indian prime minister and the Dalai Lama. In October 2013, just before former Prime Minister Manmohan Singh visited Beijing, the Chinese refused to issue valid visas for two women from Arunachal Pradesh who had been scheduled to compete at a world sporting event. The Chinese move scuttled the signing of a visa liberalisation agreement that had been in the works.

The hardening stance on Arunachal Pradesh may be attributed to China's increasing concerns about restiveness in Tibet. As the late Indian strategic affairs analyst B Raman noted in 2013, 'Beijing would like to maintain its claim to Arunachal Pradesh to justify action by the PLA in that area to contain trouble, if need be.'[5]

In addition to raising questions about the status of Arunachal Pradesh, China has called into question Indian sovereignty over the state of Jammu and Kashmir. In 2009, Beijing began stapling visas to Indian passport holders from Jammu and Kashmir. Furthermore, in July of 2010, China denied a visa to the Indian lieutenant general in charge of Northern Command, which includes parts of Kashmir. India suspended bilateral defence exchanges for about a year until

---

[3] "Text of India–China Agreement," *The Hindu*, 11 April 2005, http://www.hindu.com/thehindu/nic/0041/indiachinatxt.htm.

[4] Kanwal, Gurmeet. "India–China Strategic Relations," *CLAWS Journal*, Summer 2010, p. 143.

[5] Raman, B. "India–China Border Dispute," 22 April 2013, http://ramanstrategicanalysis.blogspot.com/2013/04/india-china-border-dispute.html.

China started issuing regular visas to Indian residents of Jammu and Kashmir.

LADAKH BORDER INCURSION PUTS INDIA ON NOTICE

The most serious border incident between India and China in over two decades occurred in April 2013 when Chinese troops settled for three weeks several miles inside Indian territory on the Depsang Plains in Ladakh. This preceded the Chinese premier's visit to India and almost led to its cancellation. Beijing eventually agreed to pull back its troops, and both sides pledged to restore the status quo ante along the disputed border shortly before Chinese Premier Li Keqiang landed in India for his first overseas visit on 19 May 2013.

It is unclear why the Chinese chose to ratchet up tensions along the border weeks before the premier's planned visit to New Delhi. The border incursion occurred about one month after the new Chinese president had assumed office. The Ladakh region is strategically important for India and includes an airbase at Daulat Beg Oldie that was established during the 1962 Sino-Indian war and which the Indians re-opened in 2008.[6] The incident may have been aimed at pressuring India to pull back on patrolling in the area. Some media reports claimed that the agreement to defuse the border flare-up involved India agreeing to remove temporary bunkers that had been used to shelter patrolling troops.[7] Other Indian analysts believe the Chinese intrusion was aimed at pressuring India to deactivate the air base at Daulat Beg Oldie and to inhibit India from further civil construction in the border areas. From this perspective, the Depsang incident was aimed at slowing Indian construction of its

---

[6] Hashmi, Sana. "India–China Stand-off in Depsang: Some Observations," *Centre for Air Power Studies Issue Brief,* 10 June 2013, http://www.aerospaceindia.org/Issue%20Briefs/2013/10%20June%202013.pdf.

[7] Chellaney, Brahma. "Why India's new border pact with China won't work," *Livemint,* 13 October 2013, http://www.livemint.com/Opinion/VbRYHcM2kc4arWI6aVeHsK/Dancing-in-the-dragons-jaws.html.

forward defences and restricting India's defensive capabilities.[8] Most Indian analysts view the Depsang incursion as pre-meditated and do not buy the argument that it was carried about by rogue People's Liberation Army (PLA) generals.

INDIA'S RESPONSE

India is responding to the Chinese moves and is seeking to reinforce its own claims in the disputed border areas by augmenting forces and constructing road and rail links along the shared frontiers. The Depsang incident almost certainly contributed to the Indian decision to move forward with a new mountain strike corps on the Chinese border. In July 2013, the Indian Cabinet Committee on Security (CCS) approved the deployment of a 50,000-strong special mountain strike corps to the eastern sector. The new corps will be called 17 corps and will be stood up over a period of about seven years.[9] This is the first strike corps India has deployed to the LAC in fifty years. Its other three strike corps are maintained near the border with Pakistan.

Three years ago India deployed two squadrons of Su-30 MKI fighter jets and raised two mountain divisions in Assam with the aim of defending Arunachal Pradesh. India also redeployed elements of its 27th Mountain Division from Jammu and Kashmir to the patch of land that intersects India, Tibet, and Bhutan and links India with the rest of its Northeastern states in 2008.[10] The Indians are building up infrastructure in the border areas, including plans for over 2,000 miles of road along the disputed border with China. India has also avoided stating its support for a 'one China' policy since 2010.

---

[8] Raman, B. "Chinese Manoeuvres against India's Possible use of the Gilgit-Baltistan Card," *C3S Paper No. 1141,* 2 May 2013.

[9] "Army gets final nod for raising corps along China border," *dnaindia.com,* 19 November 2013, at http://www.dnaindia.com/india/report-army-gets-final-nod-for-raising-corps-along-china-border-1921627.

[10] Curtis, Lisa. "US–India Relations: The China Factor."

TENTATIVE BORDER AGREEMENT

The Border Defense and Cooperation Agreement (BDCA) signed during former Prime Minister Singh's visit to China in 2013 is unlikely to significantly reduce border tensions or lead to a broader settlement in the near future. The accord is aimed at putting in place institutional mechanisms for maintaining peace along border but several Indian analysts worry that it is part of China's effort to keep in place the status quo, which favours the Chinese. Some have even contended that the Chinese intend to buy time on their border disputes with India through the BDCA while focusing on territorial claims in the Asia-Pacific.[11] To quell some of these concerns, India's former ambassador to China S Jaishankar said the agreement did not affect India's right to build infrastructure at the border.

The BDCA affirms that neither side will use its military capability against the other and proposes opening a hotline between each country's military headquarters, instituting meetings between border personnel in all sectors, and ensuring that neither side tails the other's patrols along the LAC.[12] The agreement also includes language that stipulates in the event that the two sides come face-to-face, they 'shall exercise maximum self-restraint, refrain from any provocative actions, not use force or threaten to use force against the other side, treat each other with courtesy, and prevent exchange of armed conflict.'[13] Other pledges in the agreement include increasing information sharing on military exercises and cooperation on anti-smuggling and natural disaster initiatives.

---

[11] Sandhu, PJ Major General (Retd). "Border Defence Cooperation Agreement – What Next?" *The United Service Institution of India web site*, 28 October 2013, http://www.usiofindia.org/Article/?pub=Strategic%20Perspective&pubno=38&ano=2003.

[12] Bipindra, NC. "India, China skid on visa, ink border pact," *Indian Express,* 24 October 2013, http://newindianexpress.com/nation/India-China-skid-on-visa-ink-border-pact/2013/10/24/article1852361.ece.

[13] Subramanian, Nirupama. "India, China not to use force in case of face-offs," *The Hindu,* 24 October 2013, http://www.thehindu.com/todays-paper/india-china-not-to-use-force-in-case-of-faceoffs/article5266608.ece.

FACTORING IN ECONOMICS

Despite border tensions, economic ties between China and India continue to grow. Trade dipped slightly in 2013 to USD 66 billion (it was USD 74 billion in 2012) but China remains India's biggest trading partner. China aims to take trade levels to USD 100 billion by 2015, which is noteworthy, considering bilateral trade stood at a paltry USD 2 billion just a decade ago. In January 2013, India and China held the second round of the Strategic Economic Dialogue in which the Chinese announced USD 5.2 billion worth in investments in India. The Indians complain about the USD 23 billion trade deficit in favour of China and are pushing the Chinese to open their markets for Indian goods, especially in the information technology and pharmaceutical sectors. In March 2013, Chinese President Xi Jinping said the two countries should 'harness each other's comparative strengths and expand win-win cooperation in infrastructure, mutual investment and other areas.'[14]

LOOKING EAST WITH GREATER PURPOSE

India's 'Look East' policy began in the 1990s with a focus on building economic relationships. India signed a free trade agreement (FTA) with the Association of Southeast Asian Nations (ASEAN) in 2009 and concluded talks on a services and investment FTA in 2012 to try to increase trade with the grouping from its current level of USD 80 billion to USD 200 billion by 2022. India is active in all of the main regional groupings including the ASEAN Regional Forum, the East Asia Summit, and the ADMM-Plus.[15] In the last few years,

---

[14] Kondapalli, Srikanth. "Manmohan Singh's visit to Beijing: Incremental and Institutional Progress," *www.indiawrites.org,* 30 October 2013.

[15] Lohman, Walter. "The Importance of Reality in US–India East Asia Cooperation," *Testimony before the Subcommittee on Asia and the Pacific, Foreign Affairs Committee, US House of Representatives,* 13 March 2013, http://www.heritage.org/research/testimony/2013/03/the-importance-of-reality-in-us-india-east-asia-cooperation#_ftn1.

however, India has focused increasingly on buttressing security ties with Asian nations, namely Australia, Japan, and Vietnam, to meet the challenges of a rapidly rising China.

India and Australia have slowly improved defence ties in the last several years. They concluded a Memorandum of Understanding (MoU) on Defence Cooperation in 2006 and a Joint Declaration on Security Cooperation in 2009. But it was not until December 2011 when former Australian Prime Minister Julia Gillard reversed Australia's ban on uranium exports to India that a qualitative shift in their security engagement began to emerge. In its 2013 Defense White Paper, Australia announced expansion of its principal strategic focus from the 'Asia-Pacific' to the 'Indo-Pacific', with the recognition that it must adopt a more active security role in the Indian Ocean.[16] Former defence minister AK Antony visited Canberra in June 2013, marking the first-ever visit by an Indian defence minister to the country. During the visit, the two sides agreed to start joint naval exercises in 2015.

Indo-Japanese ties have also seen marked improvement in the last few years, and are expected to get a major boost from Prime Minister Shinzo Abe, who was re-elected to power in December 2012. Abe has been a long-time supporter of stronger ties between India and Japan and initiated the idea of the Quad (US-Australia-Japan-India security grouping) during his previous tenure in 2006. Abe was also the first leader to acknowledge that the Pacific and Indian Oceans should be linked strategically on the basis of the need to preserve free and open seaways, thus coining the phrase 'Indo-Pacific.'[17]

---

[16] Brewster, David. "Australia and India: Indo-Pacific Partners," *East-West Center Asia-Pacific Bulletin Number 217*, 25 June 2013, http://www.eastwestcenter.org/sites/default/files/private/apb217.pdf.

[17] Ambassador Inderfurth, Karl F and Osius, Ted, "India's 'Look East' and America's 'Asia Pivot': Converging Interests," *US–India Insight Vol. 3, Issue 3*, March 2013, http://csis.org/publication/indias-look-east-and-americas-asia-pivot-converging-interests.

While their economic ties pale in comparison to those between China and India, Indo-Japanese diplomatic engagement has intensified. Japanese Emperor Akihito paid a rare visit to New Delhi in late 2013. The last time the royal Japanese couple visited India was in 1960. Prime Minister Manmohan Singh made a historic four-day visit to Tokyo in May 2013, in which the two sides signed a joint statement pledging nuclear cooperation and expanded joint naval exercises. Japan also endorsed India for membership in the four major multilateral export control regimes, signalling Tokyo's acceptance of India's nuclear status. Bilateral trade remains relatively low at USD 18.5 billion for 2012-13, despite the conclusion of a Comprehensive Economic Partnership Agreement that went into effect in 2011. The fifth meeting of the US-Japan-India trilateral dialogue was held in Tokyo in November 2013.

India also is pursuing better ties with Vietnam to try to check Chinese naval influence and access to the Indian Ocean. Indian officials have long understood the importance of Vietnam in the South China Sea and its potential to balance the Chinese naval presence in the Indian Ocean. In October 2011, New Delhi and Hanoi signed an agreement for India to expand oil exploration in the South China Sea. During his visit to India in November 2013, the secretary general of the Vietnam Communist Party Nguyen Phu Trong expanded the prospect for greater oil cooperation between the two countries by offering India seven oil blocks in the South China Sea. In return, New Delhi offered a USD 100 million credit line to Hanoi for the purchase of military equipment. Additionally, they signed an air services agreement to increase direct air travel between the two countries.

India has pursued oil ties with Vietnam even when China has tried to warn against them. Shortly after their 2011 agreement, Beijing questioned the legality of Indian oil exploration off the coast of Vietnam. New Delhi decided to support Hanoi's claims to sovereignty over the two oil blocks in question—blocks 127 and 128.[18] And when India, a year later, decided to abandon oil block 128, Hanoi asked New Delhi to stay on until 2014, to which India agreed.[19] Indian receptivity to Vietnamese overtures may be motivated at least in part by its desire to try to convince China to think twice before expanding its already close security ties with Pakistan.

CHINA–PAKISTAN

One of the biggest irritants in India's relations with China is Beijing's willingness to supply its arch-rival, Pakistan, with defence and nuclear cooperation that bolsters Islamabad's position in the South Asian strategic balance. China maintains a robust defence relationship with Pakistan, and views a strong partnership with Pakistan as a useful way to contain Indian power in the region and divert Indian military force and strategic attention away from China. The China–Pakistan partnership serves both Chinese and Pakistani interests by presenting India with a potential two-front theatre in the event of war with either country. Chinese officials also view a certain degree of India–Pakistan tension as advancing their own strategic interests as such friction bogs India down in South Asia and interferes with New Delhi's ability to assert its global ambitions and compete with China at the international level.

China has recently agreed to provide Pakistan two new civil nuclear reactors, even though the US and other countries have told the Chinese that the sale would violate its Nuclear Suppliers

[18] Pant, Harsh V. "India and Vietnam add a new punch to their relationship," *Business Standard*, 23 November 2013, http://www.business-standard.com/article/opinion/harsh-v-pant-india-and-vietnam-add-a-new-punch-to-their-relationship-113112300783_1.html.

[19] Panda, Ankit. "India and Vietnam Continue to Make Important Strategic Inroads," *The Diplomat*, 21 November 2013, http://thediplomat.com/2013/11/india-and-vietnam-continue-to-make-important-strategic-inroads/.

Group (NSG) commitments.[20] This action indicates that China is uninterested in working with the US to promote stability in the subcontinent and instead is focused on supporting its historical ally against neighbour India. The deal would mark the first foreign sale of this type of indigenous Chinese reactor, which has a 1,100 megawatt capacity. The two reactors are slated to be constructed near Karachi and expected to cost around USD 9.6 billion.

China helped Pakistan build two other nuclear reactors at the Chasma site in the Punjab province under agreements made before it joined the NSG in 2004. Beijing also is in the process of building two additional 350-megawatt reactors at the Chasma location (Chasma-III and Chasma-IV) that are scheduled to come online by 2016.

China seeks to expand economic linkages through Pakistan to increase commerce to the region and ultimately to the Middle East via the deep-sea port at Gwadar in Baluchistan Province. Beijing took control of the Gwadar port in February 2013. The port could allow China to secure oil and gas supplies from the Persian Gulf. But this also requires China to develop land routes through Pakistan, which is a monumental undertaking and entails security risks. In July 2013, Chinese Premier Li Keqiang and newly re-elected Pakistani Prime Minister Nawaz Sharif signed several agreements to boost their economic links, including a pledge to develop the Karakoram Highway linking Kashgar, in north-western China, to Gwadar.

A few years ago Western media reported that around 10,000 PLA troops were located in the Northern Areas of Pakistan to help carry out construction of roads and other infrastructure projects and rebuild areas devastated by the massive Pakistani floods of 2010. New Delhi is understandably wary about the presence of any Chinese troops in what is technically part of the sensitive disputed area of Kashmir.

---

[20] Curtis, Lisa. "US Should Press China to Abide by NSG Rules on Pakistanis Nuclear Cooperation," *Heritage Foundation Issue Brief #4070,* 18 October 2013, http://www.heritage. org/research/reports/2013/10/china-pakistan-and-the-nuclear-suppliers-group-commitments.

KEEPING CALCULATED DISTANCE FROM THE US

Indian concerns about a rising China do not necessarily translate into it wholeheartedly welcoming closer ties to the US. Both India and the US share a similar wariness about the military and maritime ambitions of a rising China. But turning their shared geopolitical concerns into concrete cooperation has not been easy and is often hindered by entrenched suspicions about American policies within the Indian bureaucracy.

Indian officials baulk at the idea of New Delhi serving as a counterweight to Chinese influence and power. A report released by an Indian think tank in March 2012 called 'Non-Alignment 2.0: A Foreign and Strategic Policy for India in the 21st Century' fleshed out the thinking behind the Indian reticence to look to the US to defend its interests when they are challenged by the Chinese. The report declared that it would be risky for India to rely too heavily on the US since an Indo-US strategic partnership 'could become a casualty of any tactical upswing in Sino-American ties.'[21] The report goes on to say that the American alliance system is in decline and that it is uncertain 'how the US might actually respond if China posed a threat to India's interests.' Finally, the report notes that another potential downside of focusing too much attention on building ties with the US is that it could 'prematurely antagonise China.'

Non-Alignment 2.0 spends considerable time addressing India's competition with China and the threats New Delhi is likely to face from Beijing in years to come. The report states that the 'challenge for Indian diplomacy will be to develop a diversified network of relations with several major powers to compel China to exercise restraint in its dealings with India, while simultaneously avoiding relationships that go beyond conveying a certain threat threshold in Chinese perceptions.' The report recommends building up India's

---

[21] Curtis, Lisa. "China's Rise and India's Obvious Partner (the US)," 5 March 2012, http://blog.heritage.org/2012/03/05/concerns-about-china-should-strengthen-indo-u-s-ties/.

naval capabilities to ensure it remains dominant in the Indian Ocean Region, investing in infrastructure development in the border areas, and preparing for asymmetric responses to any possible Chinese aggression regarding their border disputes.

Despite India's reticence to align itself too closely with the US, Washington and New Delhi have been taking steps to encourage greater defence trade. Former US Deputy Defence Secretary Ashton Carter discussed the possibility of the US and India co-developing the next generation of the Javelin anti-tank missile. Washington had previously baulked at joint defence production because of India's failure to sign defence technology protection agreements. Carter's announcement demonstrated that the two sides are finding ways to continue defence discussions while sidestepping the issue of technology protection agreements, at least for now. The signing of a USD 640 million deal for India to buy six additional U.S. C-130J Super Hercules aircraft also shows that the relationship still has strategic ballast. In the past five years, the US and India have concluded USD 10 billion in defence deals, but Russia remains India's top defence supplier.

CONCLUSION

Indian officials were initially cautious in their response to the US policy of rebalancing toward the Asia-Pacific. The Ladakh incursion may bring greater Indian openness to the idea of a robust US role in the region and could even prompt India to expedite purchases of US defence items and shed some of its reluctance to join more robust institutional security frameworks.

A close relationship with the US—not a military alliance—will help India maintain its long-held tradition of exercising strategic autonomy. Both countries have an interest in encouraging responsible Chinese behaviour and peaceful management of its territorial disputes. While there is still suspicion of the US within the Indian bureaucracy and a push by some Indian strategic thinkers to remain equidistant between the US and China, India will continue to rely on the US to offset growing Chinese power and influence throughout South and East Asia.

Lisa Curtis is a Senior Research Fellow, specialising in South Asia, at the Asian Studies Center at The Heritage Foundation in Washington, DC.

CHAPTER 9

The Case of the Philippines' Balancing Policy Against the China Challenge in the South China Sea

RENATO CRUZ DE CASTRO

This article examines the Philippines' efforts in intensifying its security ties with the US, its only strategic and long-standing ally. This course of action aims at strengthening the country's defence relations with the US, particularly in developing the Armed Forces of the Philippines' (AFP's) territorial defence capabilities. In this process, the Philippines finds it similarly essential to establish security ties with other US's bilateral defence partners such as Japan, Australia, and India. In conclusion, the article argues that fostering informal security arrangements with these countries enables Philippines to confront a pressing and persistent maritime issue in Southeast Asia—China's expansion in the South China Sea (SCS).

On 2 March 2011, two Chinese patrol boats reportedly harassed a survey vessel commissioned by the Philippine's Department of Energy (DOE) to conduct oil exploration in the Reed Bank, 150 kms east of the Spratly Islands and 250 kms west of the Philippines island of Palawan. Then in early June 2011, the Philippine Navy (PN) discovered a number of Chinese structures in the vicinity of Philippine-claimed Iroquois Reef-Amy Douglas Bank near Palawan and within the country's 200-nautical mile Exclusive Economic Zone (EEZ).

On 8 April 2012, the PN's flagship, the *BRP Gregorio del Pilar,* tried to apprehend several Chinese fishing boats in the Scarborough Shoal. However, two Chinese maritime surveillance vessels arrived and blocked the arrest of the Chinese fishermen who were hauling corals, clams, and live sharks into their boats. To prevent the incident from escalating into an armed clash, Philippines replaced its surface combatant with a smaller coast guard vessel. Instead of reciprocating, China deployed the Yuzheng 310—its most advanced and largest patrol ship equipped with machine guns, light cannons and electronic sensors. The Scarborough Shoal stand-off lasted for two months. It was a tense situation in which four Chinese civilian vessels confronted a lone Philippine coast guard ship. On the pretext of the onset of the rainy season, both countries withdrew their respective vessels from the shoal on 18 June 2012.

Soon after Philippines ordered its lone coast guard vessel to leave the area, China began consolidating its control over the Scarborough Shoal. The China Maritime Surveillance (CMS) ships along with the China Fisheries Law Enforcement Command constructed a chain barrier across the mouth of the shoal to block Philippine access to it. China has also deployed surveillance vessels to protect the fleet of Chinese fishing boats operating deep into the Philippines' EEZ. These incidents reflect the historic pattern of Chinese protracted, low-intensity, and incremental moves to gain control of a large portion of the SCS. China has specifically targeted Philippines in its naval brinkmanship game for obvious reasons. The country has the weakest navy in the region, and its air force cannot adequately patrol and monitor its vast maritime territory.

In confronting a militarily assertive China, Philippines adopts a delicate balancing policy. In mid-2011, it decided to pursue a substantial but much delayed modernisation of the AFP that is still preoccupied with internal security operations against domestic insurgent groups. President Benigno Simeon Aquino ordered the PN to speed up the acquisition of second-hand cutters from the US Coast Guard, and the Philippine Air Force (PAF) to scour the international market for affordable jet fighters to rebuild the country's air defence system. The Aquino administration also acknowledged the need for US diplomatic support and military assistance relative to its territorial row with China. Furthermore, the country has established informal defence linkages with the US' two allies and security partner in the region—Japan, Australia, and India. Without any credible military capabilities, Philippines finds it imperative 'to leverage' on the US and its other bilateral alliance/partners to enhance its security and develop the AFP's capabilities for territorial defence.[1]

This paper examines the Philippines' efforts to connect the Quad dialogue in the Asia-Pacific region as it establishes security ties with the US, Japan, Australia, and India to balance an emergent China. It explores this main question: How does Philippines forge defence arrangements with the US, Japan, Australia, and India? What is the Philippines' game plan in establishing security relations with the Quad countries? And how effective is this policy?

BALANCING AN EMERGENT CHINA

The 2 March 2011 incident at the Reed Bank and China's arrogant response to the Philippines diplomatic queries prompted the Aquino administration to hasten the development of the AFP's territorial

---

[1] Office of Plans and Program (J-5), Strategic Direction of AFP International Military Affairs (Camp Aguinaldo, Office of Plans and Program, May 2010). p. 2.

defence capabilities. In June 2011, the executive branch of the Philippine government and the AFP agreed on a multi-year, multi-billion peso defence upgrade spending and military build-up. The Department of Budget Management (DBM) released a Multi-Year Obligation Authority (MOA) to the DND, allowing the AFP to enter into multi-year contracts with other governments or private arms and military hardware manufacturers. The DBM also committed Php 40 billion (estimated USD 800 million) in the next five years (2012-16) to develop the AFP's capabilities for greater domain awareness of the Philippine territorial waters and EEZ.

The Philippines' territorial defence goal is to establish a modest but 'comprehensive border protection programme.' This programme is anchored on the surveillance, deterrence, and border patrol capabilities of the PAF, the PN, and the Philippine Coast Guard (PCG) that extend from the country's territorial waters to its contiguous and EEZ.[2] This objective requires prioritising the AFP's material and personnel requirements for territorial defence. The long-term goal, according to the 2011 *AFP's Strategic Intent*, is to develop the force structure and capabilities enabling the Philippine military to maintain a 'credible deterrent posture against foreign intrusion or external aggression, and other illegal activities while allowing free navigation to prosper.'[3]

The Aquino administration, however, is hampered by limited financial resources even with its modest defence acquisition goals. The PN's two former US Coast Guard Cutters are no match to China's naval prowess in the SCS. It could not immediately purchase much needed war material such as blue-water missile-armed ships,

[2] National Security Council, *National Security Policy 2011-2016* (Quezon City: National Security Council, April 2011). p. 39.
[3] Office of the Deputy Chief-of-Staff, *Armed Forces of the Philippines: Strategic Intent* (Quezon City: Camp Aguinaldo, 2011). p. 27.

search-and-rescue vessels, naval helicopters, strategic sea lift ships and top-of-the-line interceptors to protect the Philippines' oil exploration projects and maritime borders. The AFP waited so long for a bill simply extending the original AFP modernisation law (Republic Act 7898) after it expired in February 2010. In December 2012, the Philippine Congress passed the legislation and President Aquino signed Republic Act No. 10349, which extended the period for the AFP modernisation. The law, however, provides only Php 75 billion (USD 1.5 billion) for the next five years. This amount is not enough to cover the AFP's projected purchase of modern fighter planes, missile-armed frigates, sea and land-based missile systems, patrol vessels, and long-range reconnaissance planes along with support facilities such as radar sites, forward operating bases, hangar, communication, maintenance, and command and control facilities.

LEVERAGING ON THE QUAD COUNTRIES

A significant factor behind the Aquino administration's efforts to confront China in the SCS dispute, despite its military inadequacies, is the country's alliance with the US. The Aquino administration is aware that no amount of financial resources will enable Philippines to confront an assertive China in the SCS. The AFP's maritime border patrol system is designed for limited deterrence and asymmetric combat but not for naval warfare. Particularly, the PN and PAF's' capabilities for early warning, surveillance, and command, control and communication are directed towards maritime defence and interdiction operations. This build-up merely complements the deterrence provided by the US forward deployment and bilateral alliances in East Asia. In the final analysis, the Philippines' territorial defence stance is predicated upon the US's assertion of its position as the dominant naval power in the Pacific.

STRENGTHENING TIES WITH THE PHILIPPINES' ONLY STRATEGIC ALLY

The US Global War On Terror in 2001, and the tension in US–China after 2008 augured well for the Philippines' security agenda vis-à-vis an expansionist China. The revitalised Philippine–US alliance achieved two strategic objectives. One, the Philippine government received US support for its counterterrorism/counter-insurgency campaigns. Two, the US deepened its alliance with Philippines not only to neutralise terrorist groups, but also to counter Beijing's political and economic influence in the country. Consequently, the US regularly provides technical and military assistance to the AFP to firm up their security partnership against China's naval might and assertiveness. Thus, an important factor in the Aquino administration's balancing policy on China is the strengthened and reconfigured Philippine–US security relations. Currently, Washington's medium-term goal is to assist the Philippine military in its counter-insurgency/counterterrorism efforts, maritime security concerns, and transition from internal security to territorial defence. In the long-run, Washington hopes that Philippines can help maintain America's key strategic interest in Southeast Asia, a regional balance of power that tilts in favour of the US. At present, China can undermine that delicate balance of power.

Philippines maintains strong security ties with the US through the sixty-year-old Mutual Defense Treaty (MDT). Philippines regards the American military presence in the Asia-Pacific as a stabilising force, given the growing complexity of security challenges confronting the region.[4] In 2010, China's bullying behaviour in the SCS caught the attention of the US–Philippine Mutual Defense Board (MDB), the liaison and consultative body that oversees the Philippine–US

---

[4] National Security Council, *National Security Policy 2011-2016: Securing the Gains of Democracy* (Quezon City: National Security Council, April 2011). p. 16.

defence posture against external threats. The MDB annual meeting on 18 August 2010, discussed the security challenges that the allies face such as terrorism, domestic insurgency, and potential flashpoints specifically the maritime dispute in the SCS.[5] Both countries decided to complement each other's military capabilities, enhance inter-operability between their armed services, and strengthen the AFP's territorial defence capabilities with tangible US security assistance.

Consequently, Philippines and the US agreed to conduct an annual bilateral strategic dialogue. The dialogue provides an opportunity for the foreign and defence departments of the two countries 'to affirm the strength of the Philippine–US alliance and the dynamic [security] partnership for peace, security, and stability.'[6] In late January 2011, the first bilateral strategic dialogue discussed current security challenges and identified new areas for cooperation. The allies also agreed to upgrade their mutual capabilities in maritime security through the following:[7] a) US funding support to the AFP's Capability Upgrade Program (CUP), especially in the acquisition of equipment, and refurbishing and maintenance of existing AFP materiel; and b) the provision of additional funding (of USD 40 million) for the Coast Watch South project to boost the Philippine military's surveillance, communication, and interdiction capabilities in the SCS.

In November 2011, the allies signed a joint communiqué on the sixty-year-old MDT, declaring their mutual interest in maintaining the freedom of navigation, unimpeded lawful commerce, and the

---

[5] Interview with mid-level AFP Officers, Foreign Service Institute, Department of Foreign Affairs, 17 September 2010.

[6] "US and Philippines to Hold Bilateral Strategic Dialogue," *Targeted News Service* (26 January 2011). pp. 1-2. http://proquest.umi.com/pqdweb?index=63&did=2265055391&Src...

[7] Co-Chair's Statement, "Philippines–United States Bilateral Strategic Dialogue," United States Embassy in Manila, 27-28 January 2011. p. 10.

transit of people across the seas.[8] Both countries expressed their adherence to a rules-based approach that can resolve competing maritime claims through peaceful, collaborative, multilateral, and diplomatic processes within the framework of international law. The communiqué also stated that the sixty-year-old alliance has never been stronger and will continue to expand in the twenty-first century to enhance the Philippine military's defence, interdiction, and apprehension capabilities in the country's maritime domain.

The two allies held the second bilateral strategic dialogue in Washington, DC in January 2012. The aim was to 'shift the [security] partnership into a higher gear at a time when the two countries' ties have become broad-based, modern, mature and resilient.'[9] During the talks, Philippine foreign affairs and defence officials asked their counterparts for increase in US military presence in the country. They also agreed to streamline the diplomatic clearance process for US personnel and ships entering the country for combined training and interoperability. [10] Currently, the two countries are negotiating on the 'Framework Agreement on Increased Rotational Presence and Enhanced Agreement (IRP).' The IRP will facilitate the deployment of American troops and equipment on a rotational basis, and thus, circumventing the sensitive issue of re-establishing US bases in the country. Interestingly, the negotiation is conducted amidst escalating tension between Philippines and China over the SCS dispute. With its small and obsolete naval force and an almost non-existent air force, Philippines relies on US assistance to modernise the AFP's

---

[8]"Philippines–United States: Philippines, US Affirm Mutual Defense Treaty as Foundation of Relationship; Signed Manila Declaration," *Asia News Monitor* (18 November 2011). p. 2. http://proquest.umi.com/pqdweb?index=156&did=251358305&Sr...

[9]Esplanada, Jerry E. "2nd Philippine–US Strategic Dialogue set Next Year," *McClatchy-Tribune Business News* (28 October 2011). pp. 1-2. http://proquest.umi.com/pqdweb?index=1&did=2496704781&Srch...

[10]Whaley, Floyd. "Philippines in Talk to Expand US Military Ties," *The International Herald Tribune* (27 January 2012), p. 1 and 3.

defence capabilities through short-term regular visits by US forces that conduct military training as well as humanitarian and disaster response operations. More importantly, Philippines banks on the deterrent effect of the temporary deployment of US forces and equipment in its territory.

A dynamic partnership with the US enables Philippines to strategise its territorial/maritime defence through domain awareness. Therefore, Philippines must develop military interoperability with the US and execute naval diplomacy, targeted engagement, and security assistance arrangements to enhance the country's maritime security.[11] Enhanced strategic engagements with the US also require Philippines to link with Washington's other alliance/security partners in East Asia such as Japan, Australia, and India. The Philippines' 2011 National Security Policy mentioned the need to maintain security ties and to reaffirm its alliance with the US since American military presence is a major stabilising factor in the region.[12] It also proposed that Philippines must pursue its cooperation arrangements with ASEAN, Japan, South Korea, India, and Australia, among others. Meanwhile, the AFP's 2011 Strategic Intent stated that while Philippines has only one formal defence treaty (the 1951 MDT with the US), it will be beneficial for it to engage and strengthen its relationship with seventeen countries that have signed security cooperation agreements with the AFP. Australia, Japan, India, and South Korea are among those countries.[13]

The Philippines' efforts to forge security ties with Japan, Australia, and India are hedged on its strategic bets in the light of its limited military capabilities. It likewise complements the country's alliance with the US that serves as a principal deterrence against external threats.

---

[11] Office of the Secretary of National Defense, *Defense Strategic Guidance, 2013-2018* (Camp Aguinaldo: Department of National Defense, 11 October 2011). p. 18.

[12] National Security Council, *op. cit.* p. 38.

[13] Office of the Deputy Chief-of-Staff, op. *cit.* p. 34.

The 2010 Strategic Direction of AFP International Military Affairs stated that the Philippine military shall maximise gains from the alliance with the US, while seeking and developing relationship with other potential allies such as Australia, South Korea, and Japan which are key players in the Asia-Pacific region.[14] The document also confirmed that Philippines intends to develop relations with them to enhance the country's security and develop its military (specifically territorial defence) capabilities.[15]

The Philippines' plan to harness the Quad countries jibes with Washington's agenda of revitalising America's well-established alliances in Northeast Asia and deepening America's security relationship in South and Southeast Asia.[16] This is Washington's strategic response to the geo-strategic significance of the littoral states of East and Southeast Asia (from the Sea of Japan to the Bay of Bengal) which are rapidly emerging as the most politically, economically and strategically important areas. With the US strategic pivot to Asia, linking the bilateral alliances is one way of reassuring allies (especially those that are confronted by increased Chinese assertiveness on maritime disputes over the Senkaku Islands in East Asia and the Spratly Islands in the SCS) that the US has the ability and will to fulfil its security commitments in the Asia-Pacific region for decades to come.[17]

ENGAGING JAPAN IN FOSTERING MARITIME SECURITY

Historically, Philippines and Japan have maintained vigorous economic and transnational relations. Both countries adhere to

---

[14] Office of Plans and Program (J-5), *Strategic Direction of AFP International Military Affairs: Executive Summary* (Camp General Aguinaldo, Office of Plans and Program, May 2010). p. 2.

[15] *Ibid.* p.2.

[16] Denmark, Abraham M and Burton, Brian M, "The Future of US Alliances in Asia," *Global Asia 5*, 4 (Winter 2010). p. 58.

[17] Saunders, Philip C. "The Rebalance to Asia: US–China Relations and Regional Security," *Strategic Forum No. 281* (August 2013). p. 9.

democratic governance, civil and political liberties, free trade, freedom of navigation, and respect for human rights. Furthermore, they are US allies whose maritime security is threatened by China's renewed aggressiveness in its maritime domain.[18] Since 2005, the two countries have conducted the annual Political-Military Dialogue as part of Japan's overall security relations with Association of Southeast Asian Nations (ASEAN) to foster confidence-building measures and explore areas of security cooperation. In these annual dialogues, Philippines and Japan have tackled several security issues of common interests such as the situation in the Korean peninsula, China's arms-build up, the SCS dispute, nuclear proliferation in Asia, and maritime security. Japan extended emergency relief assistance when Philippines was ravaged by earthquakes and typhoons in the past. Japan has pledged to assist in the economic development of Mindanao once the peace process between the Government of the Republic of the Philippines (GRP) and the Moro Islamic Liberation Front (MILF) is concluded.

However, Japan's ability to forge closer security relations with Philippines is restrained by its pacifist 1947 constitutions. Despite this restriction, both countries share common security concerns, and thus cooperate bilaterally by: a) Enhancing maritime security through joint activities by their respective Coast Guards b) Conducting joint counterterrorism and UN peacekeeping trainings c) Countering nuclear arms proliferation and d) Facilitating the rotational deployment of forward deployed US forces in East Asia. Since 2011, Japan finds it necessary to confront China's assertiveness over a territorial dispute in the SCS in which initially, it had no direct interest.

Japan and the US made a joint declaration on 17 April 1996,

---

[18]See National Institute for Defense Studies, *NIDS China Security Report 2011* (Tokyo: National Institute for Defense Studies, 2012).

calling for closer security operations in areas surrounding Japan.[19] More recently, the 2012 National Institute for Defense Studies' *China Security Report* admits: 'Being in dispute with China over the EEZ and the boundary of the continental shelf in the East China Sea, Japan inevitably has to pay attention to China's action in the SCS.'[20] There are two other reasons why the SCS dispute worries Japan. First, if successful in intimidating the smaller Southeast Asian maritime powers, China could pose the same gambit in the East China Sea where both countries have clashing claims over the Senkaku Islands.[21] Second, China's control of the SCS and the East China Sea is part of its overall strategy of anti-access/area denial to deprive the US Navy access to China's surrounding waters, and to give the People's Liberation Army-Navy (PLAN) an access to the Western Pacific outside of the so-called First Island Chain (an imaginary line that runs from Japan's mainland to Okinawa, Taiwan and the Philippines).[22] It will be easier for the PLAN to dominate the SCS if the US Navy is not present, since the Southeast Asian claimant states cannot match Chinese overwhelming naval superiority.[23] Therefore, Japan plays a balancing role by assisting some littoral Southeast Asian states to confront China's aggressive moves. Simply, Tokyo preempts Beijing's calculation that if Chinese belligerence can end the SCS dispute, then it can similarly resolve the territorial row with Japan in East China Sea.

Japan uses three instruments to balance China in the SCS

---

[19] Sudo, Sueo. *The International Relations of Japan and Southeast Asia* (London; New York: Routledge, 2002). p. 87.

[20] National Institute of Defense Studies, *op. cit*, p. 26.

[21] Storey, Ian. "Japan Steps Up to the South China Sea Plate: Tokyo is Confronting Beijing and Increasing Defense Ties with ASEAN Members to Protect Maritime Trade," *Wall Street Journal* (09 July 2012). p. 1. http://search.proquest.com/docview.1024132884/131979D7E21C...

[22] Kato, Yoichi. "China's Naval Expansion in the Western Pacific," *Global Asia* (Winter 2010) 5, 4. p. 19.

[23] National Institute for Defense Studies, op. *cit*. p. 26.

dispute—conducting bilateral consultations with key ASEAN states, strengthening Southeast Asian maritime security, and more effectively, forming trilateral security relations with US allies in the region. Japan also teams up with other US allies to confront China's belligerency. In July 2011, the Japanese destroyer *Shimakaze*, a US Navy destroyer, and a Royal Australian Navy patrol boat conducted communication training and other naval drills near the Spratly Islands. Immediately, a Chinese analyst described this low-key US-Japan-Australia naval exercise as a 'muscle flexing show.'[24] He then accused the three countries of attempting to create an Asian version of North Atlantic Treaty Organization (NATO) which, according to him, would exacerbate the SCS dispute.[25] More notable from being US allies, both countries have common security interests.

In July 2011, then Prime Minister Yoshihiko Noda and President Aquino agreed to bolster security relations between Japan and the Philippines. After President Aquino's third visit to Japan, Tokyo and Manila announced the holding of an elevated dialogue on maritime and oceanic affairs, exchanges between Filipino and Japanese defence and maritime officials, as well as Japan's capacity-building training of the 3,500-strong Philippine Coast Guard.[26] In September 2011, then Japanese Prime Minister Naoto Kan and President Aquino issued a joint statement in Tokyo, affirming that the SCS is vital as it connects the world and the Asia-Pacific, and that peace and stability therein is of common interest to the international community.'[27]

---

[24]"Planned Drill by US in South China Sea "muscle flexing show"—analyst," *BBC Monitoring Asia-Pacific* (09 July 2011). p. 1. http://search.proquest.com/docview/875596625/13A349E 13622FC...

[25]*Ibid.* p. 1.

[26]"Japan and Philippines Strengthen Maritime Security Ties," *Jane's Country Risk Daily Report* 18, 195 (09 September 2011). p. 1. http://search.prospect.com/docview/894795349/13A38 4763AF488...

[27]Esguerra, Christian V. "Philippines Gets Japan Support on Spratly Dispute," *Tribune Business News* (28 September 2011). http://search.proquest.com/docview/894306416/13A34DA4D4 DFF70...

Prime Minister Kan also instructed the Japanese Coast Guard (JCG) to train the Philippine Coast Guard, hold consultations with Filipino naval officers, and increase joint coast guard exercises.[28]

In April 2012, at the start of the two-month stand-off between Philippine and Chinese civilian ships at Scarborough Shoal, Japanese Ambassador to the Philippines Toshio Urabe mentioned the 'close-knit triangular relationship among Japan, the Philippines, and their closest (mutual) ally—the US'[29] Then in May 2012, three surface combatants of the Maritime Self-Defense Force (MSDF) arrived in Manila for a four-day port call.[30] The visit came after Tokyo announced its plans to provide Philippines with ten new patrol vessels to bolster the latter's maritime patrol capability. The newspaper *Yomuri Shimbun* linked the ship visit to the ongoing Scarborough Shoal stand-off and editorialised that Japan could not just stand by and wait for China and Philippines to clash openly.[31] It also stressed that it is in 'Japan's national interest to ensure that its sea-lanes remain safe.'[32] Interestingly, the MSDF's ship visit to Philippines happened just a few days after the US Navy's Virginia class attack submarine, the *USS North Carolina* made a supposedly port-call in Subic Bay in Luzon. Actually, these ship visits were routine port-calls. However, they were made during the Scarborough standoff and were extensively publicised. In a sense, Washington and Tokyo were conveying a tacit message to Beijing that the two allies

---

[28] Hookway, James and Koh, Yoree, "Japan, Philippines Seek Tighter Ties to Counter China," *Wall Street Journal* (27 September 2011). p. 1 http://search.proquest.com/docview/8941257 05/13A349E13622FC...

[29] "Japan/Philippines/United States: Japan Envoy Notes Close-Knit Relations among Philippines, Japan, and US" *Asia News Mentor* (11 April 2012). p. 1 http://search.proquest.com/docview/993161337/13A384763AF88...

[30] "Philippine Navy Says Japan Sending Three Warships for Port Call to Manila," *BBC Monitoring Asia-Pacific* (26 May 2012). p. 1. http://search.proquest.com/docview/1023495 212/13A384763AF48...

[31] *Ibid.* p. 1.

[32] *Ibid.* p. 1.

would not hesitate to act collectively if the Philippines is threatened by any form of Chinese armed aggression.[33]

In July 2012, then Japanese Defense Minister Satoshi Morimoto and his Filipino counterpart, Voltaire Gazmin, inked a bilateral agreement that emphasises maritime security.[34] This agreement features high-level dialogues between defence officials and reciprocal visits by the MSDF chief-of-staff and the PN flag commander. A few days later, Philippine Foreign Affairs Secretary Albert del Rosario announced that Tokyo was likely to provide the Philippine Coast Guard with ten forty-metre boats as part of Japan's ODA to the Philippines by the end of the year.[35] Newspapers also reported that two additional bigger vessels are also being considered for transfer to the Philippine government under a grant.

In January 2013, Foreign Minister Fumio Kishida announced Japan's technical assistance to the PCG's through the provision of essential communication system equipment for maritime safety.[36] More recently, on 27 June 2013, Japanese Defense Minister Itsunori Onodera and his Philippine counterpart, Voltaire Gazmin, confirmed the continuous 'exchanges of information aimed at strengthening Philippine–Japan defence relations and on working together to make US strategic rebalancing a reality in Asia.'[37] Secretary Gazmin also

---

[33] Almazan, Alec. "US N-sub in Subic a Strong Signal to China: Routine Visit Comes amid Reports China is Mobilizing Fleet for Philippines Ops," *The Business Times* (18 May 2012). p.1. http://search.proquest.com/docview/1014157381/13914D940E373...

[34] "Japan and Philippines Sign Defense Pact," *Jane's Country Risk Daily Report* (4 July 2012) 19, 134. p. 1. http://search.proquest.com/docview/102349/13A38763AF488...

[35] Esplanada, Jerry E. "Philippines, Japan to Enhance Maritime Security Ties," *Philippine Daily Inquirer* (9 July 2012). p. 1 http://globalnation.inquirer.net/43508/philippines-japan-to-enhance...

[36] Anonymous. "Philippine/Japan: Philippines, Japan Agree to Enhance Cooperation in Maritime Security," *Asia News Monitor* (14 January 2013). p. 1. http://search.proquest.com/docview/1269104724?accountid=28547

[37] Anonymous. "Philippines, Japan Agree to Strengthen Defense Ties," *BBC Monitoring Asia-Pacific* (27 June 2013). p. 2. http://search.proquest.com/docview/137173115?accountid=28547.

raised the possibility of allowing the Japanese SDF access to the former American military bases in the Philippines if Tokyo is interested in negotiating and signing an access agreement with Manila.[38]

JUMP-STARTING PHILIPPINE–AUSTRALIA SECURITY RELATIONS

In a 2006 bilateral review, the Australian government described its security relations with the Philippines as 'very strong' and based on friendly ties, as well as common strategic interests in a secure, stable and prosperous region.[39] The two countries are formal US treaty allies that are also engaged in bilateral security relations. The two countries' navies hold an annual joint naval exercise labelled Philippine Navy—Royal Navy Exercise LUMBAS to enhance their interoperability and readiness. The Philippine Army and the Royal Australian Army conducted Land Activity Dawn Caracha which focuses on the training of special forces. The Philippines also received Australian military assistance, such as training courses for senior AFP officers in Australian military schools, and the provision of 28 flat-bottomed airboats used for both combat and disaster relief operations. Both countries also cooperate in counterterrorism training under the Philippine–Australia Capacity Building Project, which began in July 2001 during the then Australian Prime Minister John Howard. The project involves the provision of financial and technical assistance to the Philippines for law-enforcement, immigration, and port and transport security. Since 2005, Australia has provided financial and technical support to the Coast Watch South project.

In 2007, Philippines and Australia signed the Philippines–Australia Status-of-Forces Agreement (SOFA). The agreement follows the format of the US–Philippine Visiting Forces Agreement

---

[38] *Ibid.* p. 2.
[39] "Australia, Philippines to Sign Defense Treaty: Envoy," Xinhua *News Agency* (25 August 2006). p. 1. http://search.proquest.com/docview/452462495/135CBA374052DE...

(VFA) signed in 1997. The SOFA provides legal guarantees to Australian forces conducting joint-counter terrorism exercises in the Philippines. It also extends technical assistance to the AFP's logistics, and acquisition policy. The SOFA, however, does not oblige either party to assist the other in case of an armed attack by a third party. Merely, it covers issues of jurisdiction over Australian troops training in Philippines and vice-versa as the two countries undertake joint military exercises. In October 2011, then Australian Foreign Minister Kevin Rudd visited Philippines to discuss with Foreign Affairs Secretary Del Rosario key regional and bilateral matters. The two sides tackled improved cooperation on disaster response, consolidation of defence, counterterrorism measures, and mutual concerns on maritime security, such as the SCS dispute. Although Australia is not a claimant state in the South China Sea dispute, it shares with Philippines the strategic interests of 'unimpeded access to the region's maritime commons.'[40] Thus, Australia stood behind the Philippine's position with regard to the South China Sea dispute during the Philippine–Australia Ministerial Meeting in Canberra on 16 June 2011.[41]

In July 2012, after five years of intense debates and deliberations, the Philippine Senate finally ratified the agreement. The SOFA contains the detailed legal framework for Philippine–Australian military activities such as the Coast Watch South project and the Joint Maritime Training Activity LUMBAS. After the Philippine Senate ratification of the SOFA on 28 September 2012, the first joint Philippine–Australian joint exercise was held. In October 2012, the PN

---

[40]"Australia Foreign Minister to Discuss Defense Ties During Philippines Visit," *BBC Monitoring Asia-Pacific* (20 October 2011), p. 1, http://search.proquest.com.docview/89903 0868/135CB96541D630...

[41]See "Joint Philippine–Australia Statement" Philippine–Australia Ministerial Meeting, Canberra (16 June 2011), http://www.foreignminister.gov.au/releases/2011/Kr_mr_110616a.html.

and the Royal Australian Navy (RAN) conducted the twelfth annual Maritime Training Activity (MTA) labelled LUMBAS 2012 in Manila Bay. The exercise focused on maritime security training and involved both navies' ships working together to develop interoperability in communications, helicopter operations, and anti-terrorism. A month after LUMBAS 2012, the DND announced that Australia looks forward to joining the annual Philippine–US Balikatan (Shoulder-to-Shoulder) joint military exercise.[42] With improving Philippine–Australian security relations, President Aquino offered Australia a strategic partnership similar to what the country has forged with the US and Japan.[43] He commented that Philippines and Australia have been usually on the same side of issues that have confronted their respective nations during World War II, the Korean War, and the Vietnam War.[44] He also added that both countries share the same values, and forms of government, as well as face the same regional and global challenges.

EXPLORING A STRATEGIC PARTNERSHIP FOR TWO DISTANT NEIGHBOURS

Philippines and India established diplomatic relations in 1949 as both countries were driven by the ideals of Pan-Asianism and anti-colonialism. In July 1952, the two countries signed a Treaty of Friendship to strengthen their friendly relations. However, Philippines and India became distant neighbours as they adopted divergent foreign policies during the Cold War. Philippines became a close security ally of the US, while India adopted a non-aligned policy.

---

[42]Asia News Monitor, "Philippines/United States: Aussies Plan to Join Balikatan Exercise," *Asia News Monitor* (13 November 2012). p.1. http://search.proquest.com/docview/1151086998?accountid=28547.

[43]Asia News Monitor, "Philippines/Australia: Aquino says Philippines is Offering Australia a Strategic Partnership," *Asia News Monitor* (19 October 2012). p. 1. http://search.proquest.com/docview/1112912020?accountid=28547.

[44]*Ibi*d. p.2.

Furthermore, India became embroiled in a long territorial dispute with Pakistan, which became a de facto ally of Philippines in the US-sponsored Southeast Asian Treaty Organization (SEATO). The Cold War, the Indo-Pakistan rivalry, and the Philippines' security ties with Pakistan prevented any substantial interactions between these two distant neighbours. For the Philippines, India's weight and clout in the Asia-Pacific could not be felt in Southeast Asia as it had to grapple with the problem of feeding its own people, optimise its utilisation of its resources for meaningful development, and resolve its long dispute with Pakistan.[45] Thus, India may not be quite able to play a most positive role in peace and stability in the Asia-Pacific.[46] An internal Philippine government briefing paper admits: 'Due to foreign policy differences as a result of the bipolar alliance structure during the Cold War, the development of bilateral relations between the Philippines and India was stunted.'[47]

The emergence of India as a regional economic power, the global war on terror, and later, its Look East Policy led to incremental progress in Philippine–India diplomatic/security relations. In 1998, Indian Navy and Coast Guard ships began their regular port-calls to the Philippines. In March 2002, the Indian armed forces and the AFP began conducting regular intelligence exchanges marked by reciprocal visits and meetings by high-level defence and military officials.[48] India also began sending some of its military officers to the AFP service schools, primarily to the Major Service Staff College, and the National Defense College of the Philippines. In 2004, both countries agreed to convene regular security dialogues to serve as a forum for

---

[45] Pobre, Cesar P. "The Role of the Regional Powers in the Asia-Pacific Region," *Digest: A Forum for Security and Defense Issues* (3rd and 4th Quarter 2005). p. 4.

[46] *Ibid.* p. 4.

[47] Policy Studies Office, "Briefing Paper for the National Defense College of India," (Quezon City: National Security Council, 27 May 2011). p. 1.

[48] Banzon, PG. Defense and Security Engagements of the Philippines with South Asian Countries (Camp Aguinaldo, Quezon City: National Defense College). p. 15.

sharing security assessments, and reviewing and giving direction to their cooperation in bilateral/regional security and defence relations. This resulted in the convening of the first Philippines–India Security Dialogue in Manila on 12 March 2004. In the same year, five Indian naval vessels made a port-call in Manila.

In February 2006, Philippines and India signed a memorandum of agreement on defence and security cooperation during President APJ Abdul Kalam's state visit to the Philippines. The agreement formalised existing defence cooperation between the two countries that involved port-visits by naval vessels, training of military personal, intelligence exchanges, and conducting other activities that should promote closer cooperation between their respective defence departments. The agreement also raised the prospect of cooperation in their respective defence industries.[49] At that time, Philippines and India were eyeing a possible cooperation in satellite communication, ship-building and repairs, aircraft design, manufacturing and maintenance. The Philippines was also exploring the possibility of purchasing small arms, ammunition, and medicines from India.[50] Unfortunately, there has been no major arms deal between the two countries despite the initial negotiation for the Philippines's purchase of some weapons from India. This could be attributed to the wide strategic gap between the Southeast Asia's military laggard and the world's third largest conventional military armed with nuclear weapons.[51]

In March 2011, Philippines and India held the inaugural meeting for the Philippine–India Joint Commission on Bilateral Cooperation. The commission agreed on the following: a) The signing of the bilateral Cultural Exchange Program (CEP) for a year b) Establishment

---

[49] Cabalza, Chester B. "Philippines–India: Making Impressive Strides in Strengthening Ties," *NDCP Policy Brief No. 7* (16 May 2013). p. 2.

[50] Banzon, *op. cit.* p. 16.

[51] Cabalza, *op. cit.* p. 2.

of a Joint Working Group on cooperation in counterterrorism c) Reaffirming the two countries' commitment to the reforms of the United Nations, particularly the Security Council, by increasing representation of developing countries in the permanent and non-permanent categories in order to improve efficiency, representation, and legitimacy, and for it to better meet the contemporary challenges faced by the international community and d) On the basis of the 2006 RP-India Defence Cooperation Agreement, urged the early convening of the first meeting of the Joint Defense Cooperation Committee (JDCC).

In January 2012, the two countries held the Joint Defense Cooperation Committee in Manila to further strengthen their defence cooperation. Current security cooperation between Philippines and India consists of consultation and exchange of views on common security concerns such as insurgency and counterterrorism, transnational crimes, UN peacekeeping operations, military exercise and training and maritime cooperation.[52] Officers and personnel from their respective armed services participate in various specialised trainings conducted in both countries. There are also reciprocal visits by delegations from their respective defence colleges. These two distant neighbours' modest security partnership are driven by their respective national interests to promote greater trade relations, and concern over China's growing military power in the Southeast Asian region.[53]

CONCLUSION

Confronted by China's assertive expansionism in the SCS, Philippines considers it crucial and urgent to engage the US strategically. This partnership enables the Philippines to address its pressing security

---

[52] Karambelkar, Amruta. "India–Philippines Relations," Extraordinary and Plenipotentiary Diplomatist (New Delhi: Embassy of the Philippines, April 2013).p. 68.

[53] Yahya, Faizal. India and Southeast Asia: Revisited," Contemporary Southeast Asia 25, 1 (April 2003). p. 2. http://search.proquest.com/docview/205220126?accountid=28547.

concern of territorial/maritime defence through domain awareness. Noteworthy, too, is its desire to develop the AFP's interoperability with the US armed forces, and to enhance its territorial defence capability. Significantly, this revitalised security relation involves the Philippines' efforts to link with Washington's other alliance/ security partners in East and South Asia such as Japan, Australia, and India.

Philippines engages Japan in fostering maritime security as it taps the JCG in providing technical and material assistance to the Philippine Coast Guard. As part of security relations with Japan, Tokyo will provide twelve patrol boats for the PCG. A well-developed PCG is extremely important in deterring Chinese intrusion into the country's EEZ. Philippines has also signed and ratified a SOFA with Australia to enhance security cooperation with the Australian Defense Force that includes the Coast Watch South project and the joint Maritime Training Activity LUMBAS. Despite being distant neighbours, Philippines and India have forged a modest security cooperation involving consultation and exchange of views on common security concerns such as insurgency and counterterrorism, transnational crimes, UN peacekeeping operations, military exercise and training and maritime cooperation. All these efforts are aimed to strengthen the Philippines' territorial defined posture. By establishing informal security ties with these countries, the Philippines harnesses the US's other bilateral alliances and security partnership against a pressing strategic concern in maritime Southeast Asia—China's expansionist moves in the SCS.

The Philippines' efforts to harness the Quad countries together are not a tentative, short-term and knee-jerk response to a crucial strategic concern. China's emergence and design to control the SCS present the Philippines and the US a persistent, complex, and enigmatic security challenge. Simply reviving, strengthening, or transforming the Philippine–US security alliance may not be sufficient in the long run. This long-standing alliance needs to be linked with two US bilateral alliances in the Asia-Pacific/East Asia (US-Japan, and US-Australia.), and security partnership (US-India). A coordinated four-way partnership will result in the convergence of views and well-thought-out alliance policies. These policies can redound to fostering a loose association of American allies and partners in the Asia/Pacific that can pursue shared interests and values with other East Asian states. Definitely, this loose association cannot solve all the security challenges in the region. Nevertheless, it can goad the allies and partners to participate actively and increase their responsibility in managing the regional security. More significantly, it can ensure that the US remains Asia-Pacific's guarantor of security, balancer of regional power, and champion of democratic principles in the twenty-first century.

Renato Cruz De Castro is Professor at the International Studies Department at De La Salle University, Manila, and the holder of the Leopoldo Aguinaldo Professorial Chair Lecture on Philippine-Japan Relations.

Quad Plus Dialogue
Delegate List

Australian Strategic Policy Institute

CDRE (Ret.) Sam Bateman
Professional Fellow, Australian National Centre for Ocean Resources and Security

Anthony Bergin
Deputy Director

Andrew Davies
Director, Research/Senior Analyst, Defence Capability

Mark Thomson
Senior Analyst, Defence Economics

The Heritage Foundation

James Jay Carafano
Vice President, Foreign and Defense Policy Studies, EW Richardson Fellow, and Director, Kathryn and Shelby Cullom Davis Institute for International Studies

Lisa Curtis
Senior Research Fellow, Asian Studies Center

Steven Groves
Bernard and Barbara Lomas Senior Research Fellow, Margaret Thatcher Center for Freedom

Walter Lohman
Director, Asian Studies Center

Daniel Twining
Senior Fellow for Asia, The German Marshall Fund of the United States

The Tokyo Foundation

Masahiro Akiyama
President

Ken Jimbo
Senior Fellow, Regional Architecture

Ippeita Nishida
Research Fellow and Project Manager

Bonji Ohara
Research Fellow and Project Manager, Maritime Security

Ristian Atriandi Supriyanto
Research Analyst, S Rajaratnam School of International Studies, Singapore

Tsuneo Watanabe
Director of Policy Research and Senior Fellow

Vivekananda International Foundation

RN Ravi
Former Special Director of the Intelligence Bureau

Lt General (Retd.) Ravi Sawhney
Distinguished Fellow, VIF

Kanwal Sibal
Dean, Centre for International Relations and Diplomacy

Yuchengco Center

Renato Cruz de Castro
Professor, International Studies Department, De La Salle University

Additional Guests

Allen Hodges
Political Officer, US Embassy in Canberra

John Lee
Michael Hintze Fellow for Energy Security and an Adjunct Associate Professor, University of Sydney

Navarro Moore
Political Section, US Embassy in Canberra

Kensuke Yoshida
Minister, Embassy of Japan in Canberra

Index